Written by Andy Chambers, Pete Haines, Andy Hoare, Phil Kelly and Graham McNeill.
Includes excerpt from 'Execution Hour' by Gordon Rennie, used courtesy of the Black Library.

Cover Art: Karl Kopinski.   **Internal Art:** Alex Boyd, Paul Dainton, David Gallagher & Karl Kopinski.
Artwork on pages 46, 50, 54 & 58 used courtesy of the Black Library.

Editing and Layout	**Graphics**	**Models & Scenery**	**Colour Production**
Mark Owen	Nuala Kennedy & Stefan Kopinski	Dave Andrews & Mark Jones	Mark Raynor

Miniatures Painters

Neil Green, Tammy Haye, Darren Latham, Kirsten Mickelburgh,
Shaun Murphy, Seb Perbet, Keith Robertson & Chris Smart.

Miniatures Designers

Tim Adcock, Dave Andrews, Mark Bedford, Juan Diaz, Jes Goodwin,
Mark Harrison, Alex Hedström, Aly Morrison, Trish Morrison & Brian Nelson.

Special thanks to the Ancient and Honourable Order of Tech-Priests, Edward Rusk, Tim Pearce, Neil Parsons & Michael Bolton.

PRODUCED BY GAMES WORKSHOP

UK	US	Canada	Australia	Japan
Games Workshop Ltd.,	**Games Workshop Inc.,**	**Games Workshop,**	**Games Workshop,**	**Games Workshop Ltd.,**
Willow Rd, Lenton,	6721 Baymeadow Drive,	2679 Bristol Circle, Units 2&3,	23 Liverpool Street,	Willow Rd, Lenton,
Nottingham	Glen Burnie,	Oakville, Ontario	Ingleburn	Nottingham, UK
NG7 2WS	Maryland 21060-6401	L6H 6Z8	NSW 2565	NG7 2WS

Product Code: 60 03 01 02 003   Games Workshop World Wide Web site: http://www.games-workshop.com   ISBN: 1-84154-322-5

INTRODUCTION

Welcome to Codex: Chaos Space Marines. Beware, for within these pages are the secrets by which armies of the Lost and the Damned can be assembled. By reading them you risk much, for Chaos is the quick route to power and its temptations are subtle and many-fold. If you seek armies of heroes look away, for the Chaos Space Marines are the darkest of villains, traitors to the Emperor, renegades beyond redemption, motivated by power-lust and vengeance. They are also the fiercest and most brutal warriors ever known and they will continue to wage war until the Emperor is cast down and the dark gods of Chaos rule over all.

Death to the False Emperor!

Overview of the Chaos Space Marines

Long ago all of Humanity's guardians, the Space Marines, were brothers. They were all recruited from the greatest warrior peoples, all were genetically enhanced to superhuman levels, all were trained to the highest degree in the arts of war and equipped with the finest weapons. They were united in their loyalty to the Emperor of Mankind and had marched beside him on his Great Crusade to bring long-isolated human worlds into the protection of the Imperium. It was a Golden Age of great deeds and unsurpassed heroism.

Then came the apocalyptic civil war remembered as the Horus Heresy. The Imperium was sundered, every world and every institution felt the pain. At the centre of it was an act of betrayal that remains unforgiven ten thousand years later.

Fully half of the Space Marines renounced their allegiance to the Emperor. This was no mere rebellion, the Traitor Marines had fallen under the diabolic influence of the gods of Chaos, infernal warp-entities who gnaw at the edges of reality, hungry for the ripe souls of humanity's billions. The Chaos gods promised immortality and the power to indulge the Traitor Marines' deepest, darkest desires. They would be beyond punishment, with the universe theirs for the taking. Chaos beckoned and the legions of the lost and the damned followed.

They were defeated, though, by an act of supreme sacrifice on the part of the Emperor and the unflinching loyalty of their erstwhile Space Marine brothers. In defeat they were driven beyond the realms of Man into the gaping wound in reality known as the Eye of Terror. Now and forever they had become Chaos Space Marines, despised and feared as traitors and heretics throughout the galaxy. Worse still, the path to immortality offered by the Chaos gods led through a hell of death, mutation and madness. Daemonhood awaited them at the end of the road, followed by an eternity as slaves to darkness.

Still they fight on, unrepentant of the choices they have made. Taking strength from their bottomless well of hatred and bitterness, the Chaos Space Marines harness the mercurial patronage of the Chaos gods and rage ceaselessly against the Imperium and its Emperor. They will wage war without end until the Emperor is cast down and the Chaos gods rule over all.

Why collect a Chaos Space Marine Army?

There is something darkly fascinating about villains. Not the run-of-the-mill petty villains, but the big villains, the ones that plot universal domination and have the ability to see it through. These villains are just as resourceful, just as determined and just as capable as any hero but they also have faults and weaknesses that make them far more interesting. This is, I believe, the attraction of the Chaos Space Marines. There is a certain tragedy about them, but also a grim uncompromising ferocity that drives them on.

They are also incredibly diverse; from the chainaxe-wielding Berserkers of Khorne to the sorcerer-warriors of Tzeentch, each Chaos Space Marine Legion has a unique appearance and method of fighting. Armies can be built to represent just one of these Legions or an alliance of the members of several, bound together by the magnetism of an especially powerful lord. As if the Chaos Space Marines were not terrifying enough, the Daemons of the Warp answer their call to battle, thus adding another element to the armies' diversity. What the Chaos Space Marines offer you is the opportunity to build a completely distinctive army of your own. You are the writer/director of a tale of darkest villainy with complete control over the cast of characters, they can be misunderstood, aggrieved heroes pushed over the edge, consummate warriors intent on proving themselves or psychotic, nihilistic killers on a rampage, it's all up to you!

What's in the book

Army Lists: The Chaos Space Marines army list details the wargear, troop types and special rules for the Chaos Legions.

The Books of Chaos: Special rules for the followers of each of the Chaos gods, allowing you to further corrupt your Chaos Space Marines with the Marks and Gifts of Chaos.

Hobby Section: Sixteen full colour pages guiding you through the process of assembling, painting and using your Chaos Space Marine army.

Background: Information on the origins, beliefs and actions of the Chaos Space Marines, as well as the gods of Chaos themselves.

Special Characters: Tales of six of the most infamous Champions of Chaos along with rules for using them in games of Warhammer 40,000.

Codex: Chaos Space Marines and Index Astartes

The background of the Chaos Space Marine Legions has been superbly detailed in the White Dwarf Index Astartes series of articles. These articles have helped to encourage more players to build armies based around a single Chaos Legion than ever before. I was determined that this Codex should build on the Index Astartes series and that could only be done by developing a Codex that would allow any of the nine Chaos Legions to be constructed. This meant the Codex would be more rules-intensive than normal but, as the Index Astartes compilations are very much its companions, there is no shortage of background material. Some of the rules proposed in Index Astartes have had to be abandoned in order to streamline the material into the one book. The rules in this Codex supersede all rules relating to Chaos Legions printed in Index Astartes. No one should be too disturbed by this as the advantages of having all the rules in one book should more than make up for the loss of the odd quirk.

Pete Haines

Brother Janus, champion of the Black Legion, Chosen of Chaos, fired his bolter as he sprinted forwards, bright explosions of blood flaring as his shots struck flesh. He and his black-armoured warriors darted through the twilit jungle, moving and firing with methodical precision. The Crimson Fists ahead occupied a slit trench dug at the edge of their camp, with two makeshift bunkers constructed from felled trunks on each flank. They were surrounded and outnumbered, yet still refused to accept the inevitability of their defeat and the utter impossibility of victory. For ten thousand years, Janus and his brethren had butchered the servants of the false Emperor, and these tawdry progeny of the Founding Legions thought they could stand before the chosen of the gods?

Janus ducked into the cover of a thick tree trunk, enemy bolter rounds splintering its wood and showering his ornate power armour with thick, gummy sap as he slammed a fresh magazine into his weapon. He dimly remembered that the lackeys of the Emperor had once been worthy foes, but the long millennia had made them forget themselves. They were no longer the inheritors of the galaxy, merely faded echoes of their former glory. He spun low around the trunk, putting a round through the helmet of a Crimson Fist and sprinted forward. Dozens of Black Legion warriors followed him, but closer to the trenches and bunkers, the Crimson Fists' fire was more telling and more of his Black Legionnaires were falling.

Suddenly the jungle lit up, bright as day, as the bunker on the left flank exploded in a hail of white-hot plasma. An ululating howl echoed through the jungle as the mighty armoured behemoth of a blood-maddened dreadnought came into view, its plasma cannon hissing as it recharged. Its baroque sarcophagus contained the shattered remains of Amurael the Corrupted, the former leader of their band until a Khornate daemon had cleft him in two. Empires had once been claimed in his name and his

shorn torso was now fused with the arcane technologies of the dreadnought's armoured shell. The dreadnought lumbered forwards, bolter impacts ringing against its dark armour. Thick, rusted chains jangled around the mighty war machine's arms and legs, shackles that bound the bio-machine fast to its cage when not in battle.

Deafening gunfire roared from the massive weapon mounted on the dreadnought's other arm, spewing shots at a furious rate into the Crimson Fists' line. The barricades before the trench disintegrated, sending men and debris flying. The dreadnought howled with battle-lust, crashing into the enemy and hurling logs and Space Marines aside.

The Imperial flank was obliterated, the bunker burning with searing plasma fire. Janus leapt forward, the bolter kicking as he pumped shot after shot into the reeling Imperial defenders. Black Legion warriors charged the defences, leaping into the trench and hacking left and right with roaring chainswords. Janus dropped his bolter and drew his sword. He hammered his fist into the visor of a blazing Crimson Fist, whose left arm hung molten by his side. The Space Marine fell back and Janus rammed his chainsword two-handed through his breastplate.

He kicked the corpse off his blade in time to duck the lethal swing of a crackling power fist. A section of trench wall exploded under the impact. Janus rolled forwards, under the Crimson Fists Captain's reverse stroke and rose to his feet behind him, slashing his sword across his back. The Space Marine dropped to his knees and Janus spun on his heel, decapitating his foe with a single stroke. The dreadnought Amurael roared in triumph as it demolished the second bunker, the flames throwing lunatic shadows around the jungle. Janus added his howl to that of the dreadnought as the Black Legion completed the destruction of the Crimson Fists' position.

THE HORUS HERESY

The *Liber Historica Vangelia*, penned in the 34th millennium, but citing sources long since lost, traces the birth of the Imperium to the dissipation of the Warp storms isolating Terra. Around eleven thousand years ago these storms were blown away in an instant. Vangelia links this event with the Fall of the Eldar, claiming the psychic shockwave created by the birth of the Chaos power Slaanesh freed Terra from her long isolation and made possible the momentous events that followed in its wake.

That the Emperor was well prepared for the dissipation of the Warp storms is evident in the speed with which he embarked upon the reconquest of Humanity's former domain. Vast armies of human warriors, including the earliest genetically enhanced Space Marines set out in relentless waves of conquest.

Vangelia makes reference to the heroic campaigns of the period:

> *"In the name of our Lord, Ork empires did fall and noisome warrens of the Hrud were made clean. The Enslaver hold on the worlds entrapped within Warp Storm Pirithous was broken, and the Paramours of the Morpheus Rift were cast down without mercy. No pity did the Emperor show His foes, and radiant was the light of Humanity's saviour."*

Despite its momentous successes, the early years of the Great Crusade were blighted by the absence of the Primarchs. These twenty superhuman gene-sons of the Emperor were created in his geno-labs in the years prior to the dissipation of the Warp storms. A mysterious accident, or the intervention of powers opposed to the Emperor's cause had resulted in the scattering of the infant Primarchs. As the crusade continued however, the Emperor was reunited with his lost sons, discovering each upon a different human world having risen to power amongst the native population.

Each of the Primarchs was distinct in his attitudes and upbringing, yet together they formed a tightly knit brotherhood. Along with their Space Marine Legions, each of which was created using a different Primarch's genetic blueprint, they conquered the galaxy in the name of the Emperor. But it was during this time that the weaknesses, as well as the strengths of each Primarch became apparent. Although superhuman in physique, the Primarchs were all too human within their souls, and therefore fallible.

Evidently, Chaos whispered to the Primarchs as it does to all men. The difference being that where a normal man is but one mortal among billions, the Primarchs were as gods amongst Mankind, and their fall all the more calamitous. The sins that prey upon Mankind seeded themselves within the psyches of the Primarchs, and the deadliest of these was Pride.

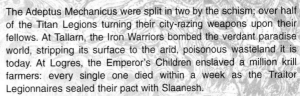

The Great Crusade had reached the Eastern Fringe, where the Emperor decided to entrust the campaign to Horus, Primarch of the Sons of Horus Legion. Horus was a consummate warrior and leader, named Warmaster of all the Emperor's armies in recognition of his formidable abilities. The Emperor returned to Terra in order to consolidate his newly won power and guide the birth of the Imperium from its homeworld.

Records surrounding the events that followed the Emperor's departure are scant at best, but Vangelia states that Horus moved against the separatist Imperial Commander of the nearby Istvaan system. Entering the system, Vangelia claims Horus wasted no time in parley or negotiation; no formal demands for surrender were made and no terms were offered. Instead, Horus unleashed a barrage of utterly lethal virus bombs upon Istvaan III. As the bombs delivered their deadly payload, all biological matter upon the surface of Istvaan III underwent a rapid degeneration. Every human, animal and plant sloughed into shapeless rotting heaps within minutes of the bombs' detonation. The gases released during the accelerated decomposition process ignited, swathing the entire world in a superheated firestorm that turned the sealed hive cities into mile-high ovens Twelve billion died that day, and the psychic feedback of their collective death scream reverberated throughout the Warp, echoing through the eternal realm of Chaos and drowning out even the pure light of the Astronomicon.

The instant Istvaan III died the Emperor knew something terrible had occurred.

The Emperor dispatched seven Legions to confront Horus, to call him to account for his actions. The Warmaster's forces had redeployed to Istvaan V, where the first wave of loyalists made planetfall. The details of what has become known as the Istvaan V Drop Site Massacre are vague, for only a handful of Space Marines survived, and their descendants will not speak of it. According to the Mythos Angelica Mortis, the Raven Guard, Iron Hands and Salamanders Legions made up the first wave of the action, and were caught off guard by the ferocity of the traitor counter attack. As the first wave became pinned at the drop site, they attempted a breakout, only to discover that the four Legions of the second wave, listed in the Libra Historica as the Iron Warriors, Emperor's Children, World Eaters and Death Guard, had betrayed them.

The loyalists were slaughtered almost to a man, trapped between the armies of Horus and the newly revealed traitors of the second wave.

In the wake of the Drop Site Massacres the Imperium tore itself apart in a galaxy-wide civil war. The empire for which so many had sacrificed so much was cast down overnight. The Space Marine Legions were split and brother fought brother in a war rooted in insanity. The ferocity of the conflict was unmatched in any bloodshed before or after. The bitterness with which a man fights his own kin is far more savage than any war he may persecute against a stranger.

Upon a million worlds, leaders who had sworn fealty to Terra renounced their vows. Governments that had been co-opted into the fold of the Imperium now threw off the shackles of what they saw as an unjust and unworthy rule, regressing to their pre-Imperial states. Where once the rule of the Emperor prevailed, now chaos and anarchy reigned.

Upon thousands of worlds the previously hidden followers of Chaos rose up. The Traitor Legions rampaged across the galaxy committing acts that bore testimony to their new loyalties.

The Adeptus Mechanicus were split in two by the schism; over half of the Titan Legions turning their city-razing weapons upon their fellows. At Tallarn, the Iron Warriors bombed the verdant paradise world, stripping its surface to the arid, poisonous wasteland it is today. At Logres, the Emperor's Children enslaved a million krill farmers: every single one died within a week as the Traitor Legionnaires sealed their pact with Slaanesh.

Horus and his hordes pushed on from sector to sector, inexorably fighting their way towards the Segmentum Solar. Recovering from their initial surprise, loyalist forces began to oppose the traitors. Spearheaded by loyal Space Marines and Titan Legions, the Emperor's forces contested world after world. Just as the loyalists began to make serious headway however, Horus demonstrated his strategic brilliance once more.

Horus had intended all along to strike a single, decisive deathblow against the Imperium, and he meant to do so at Terra. When the attack came, the loyalists found themselves woefully unprepared: Horus' cunning became even more apparent as the majority of the Emperor's Legions found themselves too far from Terra to intervene in time.

The Siege of the Emperor's Palace was the very darkest hour of Human history. The skies were turned black with Chaos drop pods and Dreadclaw Assault craft, and only three loyal Legions stood at the Emperor's side to oppose them.

The Emperor had always been guided by his innate prescience, but the future beyond this day was hidden from him. Then, at the very moment of the Warmaster's victory, Horus lowered the shields protecting his ship. Whether Horus was driven to do so by some last vestige of regret, or whether he simply wished to send his psychic sight to witness his father's death will never be known, but in the instant the shields were lowered, the Emperor became aware of the traitor's presence, and saw what must be done. Gathering his immediate companions, the Emperor, the Primarchs Sanguinius and Rogal Dorn, and a select group of warriors teleported directly to the Warmaster's battle barge. The dropping of the shields allowed one last opportunity at salvation. The final, desperate gambit was made as time ran out for the Human race.

Upon Horus's ship the Emperor and his warriors found themselves separated, each forced to confront a sea of Warp-spawned horrors alone. At length, the Emperor fought his way to the bridge, only to find Horus standing over the broken body of his brother Sanguinius, Primarch of the Blood Angels Legion. Turning, Horus faced his creator, and in an instant the two were engaged in a battle likened to that between gods.

The Emperor triumphed. He slew his most beloved son, destroying utterly his presence in the Warp and casting his blasted form to the deck. But the Emperor had paid the highest price for his victory, and death overcame him as he finally allowed his body to suffer the terrible wounds Horus had inflicted.

The battle for Terra, the Imperium, and the fate of Mankind was won, but at a terrible cost. The Emperor's wounds were so horrific that only his ascension to the arcane life-support systems of the specially constructed Golden Throne could hold his death at bay. Terra was a ruin; her cities levelled. So deep were her wounds that the tectonic plates groaned under the punishment inflicted by the traitors' orbital bombardment. The routed hordes of Chaos had left such utter devastation in their wake that nothing short of the complete rebuilding of Terra, and of the Imperium itself, would even begin to heal the wounds inflicted during the Horus Heresy.

The Heresy may have failed in its objective of replacing the Emperor's rule with that of Horus, but it had brought the realm of man to within an inch of total annihilation. The Imperium was in tatters, and as the Traitor Legions retreated to the Eye of Terror, they knew that they would return, that they would rise again. Amongst them was Abaddon, Captain of the First Company of the Sons of Horus; he took with him the body of the Warmaster and an unquenchable appetite for vengeance. The Long War had begun, and the Traitors vowed they would wage it for all eternity to see their hatred satisfied.

THE WARP

The Warp – Warp Space – The Immaterium – The Empyrean – The Ether – The Realm of Chaos

"When I open my Warp eye I look upon the face of the Empyrean and see hell itself gazing back at me. Superimposed over the mundane world I see the sharks of the Warp circling each person I regard. Those with the Sight, such as Astropaths, pyskers and my own people, Navigators, shine with a soul-fire so bright they all but obliterate the small flickers of those nearby. These attract the most voracious of Warp-bound predators, who snarl and snap and slaver from their realm. Were these individuals not protected by their own powers or their bonding to the Emperor then these creatures of the Warp would pierce their very minds and claw their way through into the material universe. This is why I cannot uncover my Warp eye in the presence of the unprotected. To meet the Warp-gaze of a Navigator is to see reflected in it the most awful of truths: that the human soul is but a mote adrift upon the ocean of the Warp, surrounded by slavering horrors from our very worst nightmares."

– Baron des Champ,
Principle of House des Champ of the Navilis Nobilite

It is said by those psyker-mystics and astral-seers who will speak of such things, that the Warp exploded into being at the same instant as the material universe, and that the two realms are inextricably and permanently linked to one another. As real-space is a dimension of the physical, so it is said, Warp space is a dimension of the spiritual.

The greatest and most prolific writer on the subject was the heretic Elijah of Mephisto V, who was very publicly executed by a conclave of Inquisitors at the turn of the 37th Millennium. Elijah's writings were often esoteric to the point of heresy, and were so couched in mysticism that few scholars could unravel their meanings. Elijah refers to the laws governing the Warp as being quite different to those governing the physical universe, if indeed any laws can be said to apply to the Realm of Chaos. He refers to the Warp as an ever-shifting dimension of raw, unfocused energy, attempting to put into words what can never be described by any sane man:

"The forces of Warp space rage like the mightiest ocean, and if a mortal could perceive the sound of that realm, he would hear every noise in the universe voiced simultaneously, and would be driven utterly and profoundly insane by the experience."

Various suppressed sources refer to Mankind as a psychically attuned race, every single human being having a presence in the Warp; a mere spark of light against an inferno. Elijah, and several other authors, insist that Man has yet to complete his transition into a being in full control of his psychic potential, and that whilst this evolution is incomplete those individuals who develop psychic powers act as a beacon to the denizens of the Warp, and the material realm

is endangered. Only the ritual soul-binding to the Emperor can protect many psykers from the perils of the Warp, and only the strongest can hope to face its terrors alone.

With the emergence of Man as the dominant race in the galaxy, the Warp, according to Elijah, underwent a parallel development. As the souls of the psychically attuned races are linked to the Warp, so their thoughts and emotions are reflected there. In his later works, which rapidly degenerate into little more than the insane ravings of a man condemned by his own knowledge, Elijah attempts to describe the nature of the Chaos powers. He claims that, in the deepest eddies in the ocean of the Warp, are formed consciousnesses, created by the emotions of the 'young races' that echo their deepest passions. Sometimes these concentrations coalesce into entities that draw their power from the expression of certain emotions in real-space. Many such beings are said to exist within the Warp, some only for a short time as the passion associated with their creation passes. Yet others have transcended the limits of their birth and are no longer mere reflections of the mortal psyche: they now have the power to inspire and feed those emotions that give them their identity; these beings are the Chaos gods, beings of incomprehensible and terrible power and they form the ultimate threat to a man's soul.

To Man, the Warp is his greatest hope, and his gravest peril. Humanity's link to the Warp enables him to draw upon the infinite power of that realm, yet his presence there, however insignificant against the incomprehensible vastness of the Realm of Chaos, draws the attention of the beings that lurk within. Until the human race has fully mastered its psychic potential it will continue to be preyed upon by the powers of Chaos which are, tragically, the product of Mankind's own imperfect psyche.

And all the while the boundless power of the Warp writhes at the borders of human perception, fuelling the dark-fire that burns within the soul of every mortal…

The Eye of Terror

Ten thousand years ago the galaxy bore witness to the Fall of the Eldar. As with so many mortal races, the Eldar soul is flawed, possessed of a dark intensity that compels it to excess in all it pursues. This led to the slow breakdown of Eldar society as each individual pursued his own passions to the exclusion of all else.

At the heart of the Eye of Terror lie the crone worlds: the original homelands of the Eldar people. These worlds are the domain of daemons and lunatics, but are also the only source of the material used by the Eldar to create their spirit stones: repositories for the Eldar soul to shield it from the eternal thirst of Slaanesh. Some Eldar still travel to the crone worlds in search of this raw material, which is said to have been formed of the raw stuff of chaos at the moment of the Fall. Few of these individuals ever return.

The Eldar will not describe their downfall to any member of a 'lesser race', but much of the story can be gleaned from what passages of Eldar mythology are known to outsiders. Throughout the long period of decline, the intensity of emotion generated by the Eldar's excess began to coalesce within the Warp. A new power was being formed, growing stronger with every indulgence, slowly forming into a vast, yet sleeping intelligence. This entity dozed fitfully, its dreams fed by the Eldar's deeds. These dreams leaked back to the Eldar psyche, and the race was plunged into further depths of evil by the insane nightmares.

In time, the Eldar people sank to the lowest depths of depravity and in an instant the sleeping power awoke. The Chaos god Slaanesh was born and its birth cries decimated the race, drawing the spirits of billions of Eldar into the Warp to be consumed by the newborn god. The entire Eldar race was devastated, but the worst destruction occurred at the heart of their galaxy-spanning empire, where the Warp erupted forth into real-space. An area almost twenty thousand light years across was engulfed in the very stuff of Chaos. This area is today known as the Eye of Terror.

Real-space is prone to warp storms; areas of space where the Warp encroaches upon reality, isolating entire systems for many years at a time. The Eye of Terror is to one of these naturally occurring warp storms as a hurricane is to a gust of wind. The Fall created an area of warp/real-space interface, a vast, open wound upon the fabric of reality constantly weeping filth and corruption. The powers within the Empyrean have direct influence within the Eye, making it a region where the laws of physics hold no sway and worlds are shaped entirely on the whim of mad gods.

The Eye of Terror is known to be home to the darkest evils of the galaxy. At the height of the Horus Heresy the Traitor Legions were driven from Holy Terra and naturally sought shelter within that Realm of Chaos. Each Legion claimed for itself a new homeworld, moulding it to its own perverse designs. The followers of the different Chaos powers fight one another in an eternal struggle for supremacy for the 'natural' resources to be found within the Eye of Terror, but they are at their most deadly on the very rare occasions when they cease fighting one another and turn their attentions to the material universe outside the Eye. Few have managed to unite the disparate factions in this manner, but Abaddon is such a being, moulding the Traitor Legions, mutant armies and Daemon hordes into his Black Crusades. These invasions are often short-lived, as few but the strongest servant of Chaos can exist for long at any distance from the twisted energies of the Warp. Only the hideous death tolls inflicted during the Black Crusades can maintain the forces of Chaos, and that death toll is always unimaginably high.

The Eye of Terror has provided the means by which the Traitor Legions have terrorised the Imperium for ten thousand years, as time within that twisted realm is as distorted as it is within the Warp itself. Ten millennia after the events of the heresy, the very same traitors who fled from the armies of the Imperium still embark upon their Black Crusades.

> *Though my guards may sleep and ships may rest at anchor, our foes know full well that big guns never tire.*
>
> *Lufgt Huron, the Tyrant of Badab.*

The Maelstrom

Located approximately forty thousand light years to the galactic east of Terra, the Maelstrom is an area of space riven with warp storms so intense that stellar travel in the region is all but impossible. Unlike the Eye of Terror, the Maelstrom is, as far as Imperial scholars can ascertain, a naturally occurring phenomenon.

With travel so difficult, the entire region has become a haven to the pirates, criminals and renegades of the galaxy. Space within the Maelstrom is a lawless wilderness containing an estimated twenty plus Ork empires, numerous Hrud infestations, and countless human pirate strongholds. It is also said to house a large contingent of Word Bearers Chaos Space Marines who fled there in the wake of the Horus Heresy. The region swirls with warp-energies that permeate its worlds, the evil of Warp space slowly poisoning those mad enough, or desperate enough, to reside within.

At the time of the Great Crusade, the Emperor's armies attempted to penetrate the Maelstrom and cleanse it of the evils lurking within. Hundreds of warships and thousands of troops were lost in the campaign, and with the rest of the galaxy to re-conquer, the Emperor declared the region Purgatus. In the years following the Horus Heresy, Roboute Guilliman decided that the inhabitants of the Maelstrom were too great a threat to the stability of the fledgling Imperium to ignore, and ordered the surrounding regions reinforced in an effort to contain any attacks that may originate from within. Initially the main responsibility for the security of the sectors bordering the Maelstrom fell to the White Scars Space Marine Chapter, whose homeworld of Mundus Planus was situated relatively close by. By the middle of the 36th Millennium however, it was plain that even the White Scars could not react fast enough to counter every threat to such a large region of space. The Senatorum Imperialis declared a new Space Marine founding in 598.M35, and one of the Chapters created in this founding was the Astral Claws, whose sole responsibility it would be to guard the space-lanes surrounding the Maelstrom and to interdict any renegades fleeing to the region to escape Imperial justice.

Of the reasons for the Astral Claws' later fall from the Emperor's grace, little is known other than the details of the sad conflict that followed as several other Space Marine Chapters sided with the Astral Claws against the Chapters sent to quash them. The Chapter's Master, Lufgt Huron declared himself above the rule of Terra and set his Chapter upon the road to damnation. Whether the rebellion was caused by the Chapter's proximity to the warp storms and the insidious influence of Chaos that seeps from them may never be known, but in the wake of the Badab Uprising, as the conflict became known, the Astral Claws and rogue elements of several other Chapters fled to the heart of the Maelstrom. There they carved themselves an empire and established themselves as cruel reavers plaguing every Imperial shipping route within 5,000 light years of the Maelstrom. Lufgt Huron renamed himself Huron Blackheart and his Chapter the Red Corsairs, and sold his soul to the undivided power of Chaos. To this day, many of those few Space Marines who tragically fall to the lure of Chaos are to be found within the ranks of the Red Corsairs, embittered and twisted by the evil power of Chaos that leeches from the Maelstrom.

LET THE GALAXY BURN

THE BLACK CRUSADES (mid M30 - present)

In the wake of the Traitor Legions defeat at the Siege of the Emperor's Palace, they fled to the Eye of Terror where they initiated a series of highly self-destructive internecine wars. It was not until the middle of the 31st Millennium that they again presented a threat to the Imperium. Abaddon, uniting the Traitor Legions under one banner led the first of his 'Black Crusades' out of the Eye of Terror. Utilising the relative calm in the warp storms in the area known as the Cadian Gate, his armies fell upon the Imperial worlds surrounding the Eye with a savagery born of the conflict that had sundered the bonds of brotherhood between the Space Marine Legions. Finding the region ill-prepared for their attack, the forces of Chaos slaughtered millions in the first weeks of the first Black Crusade. Entire populations were sacrificed to the ever-hungry daemons of the Warp, and armies wiped out to a man by the maddened Traitor Legions. It was only at the expense of scores of Imperial worlds that Abaddon's hordes were repulsed. In the wake of the first Black Crusade the Imperium was forced to fortify the entire region, turning the world of Cadia itself into a permanent garrison, and importing millions upon millions of Imperial Guardsmen into the area. The Liber Astartes, compiled in M37, lists twenty Space Marine Chapters that were founded over the following centuries with the specific role of guarding against future Chaos incursions.

In the ten thousand years since the Horus Heresy, the Traitor Legions have pursued a constant campaign of bitter warfare against the Imperium. Abaddon himself has led a total of twelve Black Crusades, ranging in scale from raids carried out by small, elite companies of Black Legionnaires, to great invasions in which all of the Traitor Legions are united under a single banner, and accompanied by massive, slavering hordes of daemons and mutants. On each occasion, the Imperium has been able to repulse the hordes, though barely, and with each Black Crusade thrown against the Cadian Gate, the Imperium's defences come closer to breaking.

Abaddon is not the only Chaos lord to lead invasions out of the Eye though: many warleaders and Daemon Princes have the resources to threaten the Imperium. In each case the force must first find a way of circumventing, infiltrating, or breaking through the Cadian Gate if it wishes to penetrate Imperial territory. Frequently, the agents of Chaos will sow anarchy and discord in order to prepare the way for an invasion, and when it comes the forces of the Imperium find themselves hard pressed on many fronts. In this way, Chaos fleets and warbands inflict death and destruction upon worlds many light years away from the Eye of Terror, and in many cases their sole objective is to inflict as much pain as possible before escaping back to the Eye carrying whatever slaves and booty they can acquire.

THE FIRST WAR FOR ARMAGEDDON 444.M41

The Imperium, and the galaxy as a whole, is in a state of perpetual war; and it can be guaranteed that where there is death and destruction, the followers of Chaos will not be far away. In the middle of the 41st Millennium, these followers brought about the invasion and near total destruction of one of the Imperium's most strategically important worlds.

Armageddon lies some 9,000 light years to the galactic south-east of Cadia but, despite this relative proximity, was at that time yet to suffer the full attentions of the Chaos hordes. This all changed when an increase in local warp storm activity coincided with the onset of

armed rebellion in the hive world's manufactory-cities. Such rebellion is not unusual, even on the most ordered of Imperial worlds, and so native planetary defence forces were left to deal with the situation as they saw fit. Unfortunately, the rebellion turned out to be a precursor for a massive Chaos invasion, and as the warp storm activity increased, a huge space hulk appeared in the Armageddon system, and disgorged a millions strong horde of possessed Daemonhosts, cultists and mutants upon the unprepared world. The Daemon Prince Angron, Primarch of the World Eaters Traitor Legion led the horde, falling upon the defenders with a bloodlust that no mortal could hope to oppose. In the first weeks of the war, countless millions lost their lives as the mass of Daemonkind and Chaos-infected humanity rampaged across the surface of the world's main continents.

Fortunately for the defenders of Armageddon, Angron's power was dependent on the nearby warp storm activity, and during a lull in the storm, the defenders were able to launch a desperate counter-attack led by a company of Grey Knights. They confronted the Daemon Prince in the very midst of his horde. The battle was of a scale not witnessed since the Siege of the Emperor's Palace, and by its conclusion the Grey Knights had paid a terrible price in the lives of their finest warriors. But Angron was banished back to the Warp, and the war was won, though Armageddon and its people suffered horribly for their freedom.

This was but the first invasion to afflict the Armageddon system. Five hundred years later the region fell under the shadow of the Ork warlord Ghazghkull Mag Uruk Thraka. That Armageddon is a focus for the forces of death and destruction is clear; Angron's invasion was but the first of three wars that have devastated this cursed world.

THE GOTHIC WAR 139-160.M41

The most devastating incursion of recent times occurred when Abaddon led a huge force against the Gothic Sector. In a war that lasted almost twenty years, and engulfed an entire region of space, Abaddon led his armies with the aim of capturing the ancient alien edifices known as the Blackstone Fortresses. Abaddon was only repulsed at great cost, but it was reported that he escaped the final battle with two of the mysterious and powerful artefacts. What blasphemous use the Despoiler intends to put these potentially devastating weapons to remains to be seen, and states of readiness in the regions surrounding the Eye of Terror have been increased accordingly.

THE LONG WAR

The Legions continue to pose a terrible threat to the Imperium, and almost every system within 500 light years of the Eye of Terror is home to an Imperial presence of one form or another. This presence ranges from the smallest listening post staffed by a handful of Tech-adepts and defended by a single platoon of Guardsmen, to the frontier worlds of the Cadian Gate where millions of men are under arms, entire continents are fortified and Imperial Navy battlegroups form impenetrable blockades. To live on these worlds is to be schooled in the arts of war from infancy, as entire planetary populations stand ready for mobilisation at the first sign of an incursion through the Cadian Gate.

The defences surrounding the Cadian Gate are tested more each year. Lonely observation stations circling barren worlds train their machine spirit guided augurs on the Eye of Terror, ever watchful for the smallest sign that the next Black Crusade is coming. Upon Cadia and a hundred other frontier-fortress worlds, billions of soldiers avert their sight from the baleful light of the Eye as it dominates the night sky of every world in the entire cursed region.

Mesmerised, the Despoiler watched as the planet below entered its final death throes. Its oceans had boiled off into space hours ago, laying bare the broken and dried expanses of once hidden sea-beds. Everywhere, bright lines of fire criss-crossed the planet's surface; rivers, lakes, entire oceans of molten magma flowing up through gaping, bleeding rents in the planetary crust as the planet itself began to break apart. The whole southern hemisphere was ablaze, covered in magma as the planet's molten heart bled out of the continent-sized open wound that the Despoiler's Planet Killer weapon had burned into it. Giant earthquakes shook the planet from pole to pole, forming and then reforming its burning topography into an ever-changing series of different, fiery visions of hell. The planet's biosphere was gone – its oxygen-rich atmosphere had ignited at the first firing of the Planet Killer's awesome weapons systems – and Abaddon assumed that all life on the world was now extinct. Perhaps a few had survived the initial firestorms that had scoured clean the surface, hiding in shelters deep below the ground, but nothing could have survived the resultant seismic catastrophe as the Planet Killer's coruscating energy beams tore apart the planetary crust and ripped deep into the underlying rock strata, finally cutting through into the planet's molten core.

Abaddon smiled, remembering other such moments of triumph, other such spectacles of destruction. He remembered standing by the side of Horus on the bridge of the Warmaster's battle barge, watching as wave after fiery wave of bioweapon missiles were unleashed at the surface of the world below them. Twelve billion people died in moments during the Scouring of Istvaan III, and the echoes of their mental death-screams had drowned out even the constant warp pulse of the Astronomican, but it was only a prelude to the devastation to come. "Let the galaxy burn," ordered the Warmaster, and Abaddon and the other commanders of the Space Marine Legions who flocked to the Warmaster's cause had done as commanded. Abaddon remembered worlds in flames, planetary systems choked with the drifting wreckage left in the wake of cataclysmic space battles, battlefronts thousands of miles long as unbroken lines of Space Marines and the towering war machines of the Collegia Titanica clashed with their one-time brethren on a thousand different worlds, under the light of a thousand different suns. He remembered the howl of triumph from a million Chaos-altered throats as he, Abaddon, First Chosen of the Warmaster, led the sweeping charge over the crumbled ruins of the outer walls of the impostor Emperor's refuge on Earth and into the sanctum of the Inner Palace itself.

A tremor ran through the metre-thick ceramite decking beneath Abaddon's feet, reverberating with a dull boom throughout the armoured hull of the massive vessel and interrupting the Despoiler's reverie.

"Warmaster," bleated a hunchbacked heretic tech-priest thing, shuffling forward to bow before the Despoiler. "The planet's core is beginning to break up, causing unpredictable and powerful fluctuations in its magnetic field." It paused, twin worm-tongues nervously flicking out to lick at canker-eaten lips. "Perhaps it would be wiser to order the vessel back to a point beyond the area of danger."

The Despoiler hissed in irritation, his thoughts disturbed by the intrusion of the minion-thing now cowering at his feet. Sensing its master's mood, his sword shivered in its scabbard, eager to be unleashed and fed. Abaddon laid a reassuring hand on the skull-carved pommel of the sheathed weapon, soothing the mood of the daemon-thing bound into the warp-forged metal of the blade. Also sensitive to their master's mood, one of the hulking, armoured figures of Abaddon's Terminator bodyguard stepped forward, crackling lightning claws sliding out with a low, buzzing sound from its armoured fists as it prepared to remove the source of its master's irritation.

Another tremor ran through the deck, underlining the tech-priest's words, and through the viewing port Abaddon saw a gout of fiery magma hundreds of miles long spurting up from the burning surface and exploding high in orbit above the dying world.

At a curt gesture from Abaddon, the bodyguard stepped back to rejoin the circle of silent warriors standing round the edge of the chamber.

Whimpering in terror, the tech-priest thing scampered gratefully away back into the safe anonymity of the surrounding shadows.

Turning his back on the viewing port behind him, Abaddon strode into the centre of the chamber, his bodyguard effortlessly moving to reform in a protective circle around him. Tech-priests, acolyte attendants and mewling chaos spawn abominations scuttled out of the crushing path of the armoured giants.

At another gesture from the Despoiler, the central section of the floor of the viewing chamber began to descend down through the lower decks of the vessel. Abaddon's unspoken command was already spreading through the length of the massive Planet Killer vessel, and as the open elevator platform rumbled downwards, those upon it could see the frenzied activity as the ship's crew hastened to act on those orders. Beyond, Abaddon knew, the crews of the ships making up his Planet Killer's escort fleet would be doing likewise, their relieved captains no doubt offering up quiet prayers of thanks to the Powers of the Warp as they manoeuvred to move their vessels away from the violent and unpredictable death throes of the doomed planet.

It was forbidden on pain of death for any of the vessel's thousands of slave workers to look upon the face of the Despoiler, and, as the platform descended through the main crew decks, snarling overseers rushed to assure immediate obedience amongst the work-crews of prisoners under their command. Already recognising the tell-tale sound of the descending elevator, many of the slaves cowered in terror, gaze fixed at their manacled feet and their endless slave work momentarily abandoned, as the platform and the dread figure standing upon it moved past them. Others continued working, raising faces in silent question at the sound of the platform's passing, and showing dark empty holes where eyes should be. Assigned to tasks where eyes were deemed unnecessary, these poor wretches had had their sight brutally taken from them by the hands of their overseers.

One chain-gang member, his still intact Imperial Navy officer's uniform showing him to have been only recently captured and enslaved into the Warmaster's service, either ignored or did not understand his overseer's barked warnings. Risking a glance towards the platform as it rumbled past, he was quickly smashed to the ground by the figure of a slavemaster wearing the dripping sigil-daubed power armour of a World Eaters Chaos Marine. Snarling in rage, the World Eater brought its chain-axe up and in one swift blow summarily decapitated the screaming slave. With solemn ceremony, it reached down to pick up the severed head, holding it up in salute to the passing figure of the Despoiler, the slave's dead eyes now permitted to gaze upon the sight that had been forbidden to them in life.

Thus did Abaddon the Despoiler, Warmaster of the Legions of Horus, commander of the so-called 'traitor legions' as the servants of the false Emperor called them, pass through the midst of his followers. Not caring whether they lived or died, not caring whether they served him through devotion, just as long as they served him first through fear.

From the novel Execution Hour
By Gordon Rennie

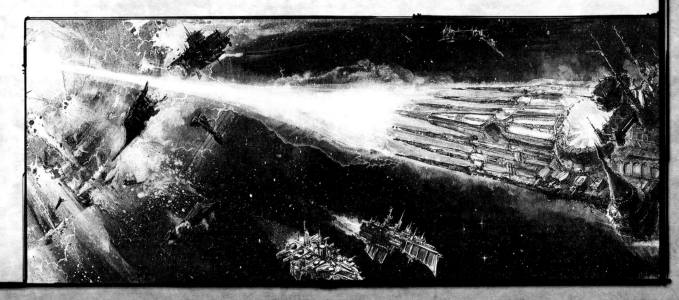

The lights were kept dim, the revolving holo-slate glowing softly with the blurry images of the targets his team were to kill. The instructor paced the room, hands laced behind his back as he waited for the ancient logic engine to unlock the encrypted files. A soft chime sounded and their mission briefing scrolled across the base of the slate. The Instructor stood before the hand-picked assassins and said, "The Chosen of Abaddon. These targets are classified threat level omega."

He was pleased to note the absence of fear in the assassins he had assembled for this mission. Each one knew that code omega meant that few, if any, were expected to survive this mission.

A giant in bloodstained black power armour swam into focus on the holo-slate, his helmet crowned with blades and a long, curving sword gripped in both hands. "The primary target is known as Devram Korda, and is believed to be the same individual once known as the Tyrant of Sarora. It is said that he distilled the bodily essences of the planet's largest hive city for a single vial of elixir. The properties of this elixir are unknown, but for a period after its ingestion, Korda became, to all intents and purposes, invulnerable. He conquered the entire system and ruled it with an iron fist, distilling yet more elixirs from the bodies of each planet's population until finally he was toppled by warriors we believe to have been rival Chaos Space Marines from the Emperor's Children."

The image faded, to be replaced by another figure in power armour, its surfaces alive with writhing sigils and carved with graven symbols. An iridescent cloak of feathers shrouded much of the hunched figure, and its face was hidden behind a leering golden mask.

"The Sorcerer, Ygethmor the Deceiver," continued the instructor, "believed to be the cause of the Corrialis system massacres. Two hundred years ago, the entire populations of six worlds in the Corrialis system, over six billion souls, died in a single night of ritual suicide. It is suspected that Ygethmor initiated a doomsday cult that spread to every inhabited world in the system and that he was in some way able to harness the power released by the mass death. Current intelligence on Ygethmor's whereabouts puts him on one of Abaddon's battle barges, though not that of Zaraphiston, as it is believed that the two are rivals for the traitor Warmaster's patronage."

The instructor paused, staring through the holographic image of the sorcerer at the assassins.

"It is likely that Ygethmor knows you are coming, but it is suspected that he will not interfere with your mission as he has much to gain should you eliminate his rivals. This, however, is speculation, not fact. All mission parameters are to proceed as though his intervention is inevitable."

Once more the image on the holo-slate shifted and two more figures appeared. The first was a warrior clad in black and bronze armour with a long glaive clutched in one gauntleted fist. His armour was archaic, each greave, vambrace and shoulder guard edged in grinning skulls. His visor was moulded in the form of a snarling wolf and the horns to either side appeared to be more a part of the warrior's head than his helmet. Accompanying the warrior was a loathsome, twisted creature, its scabrous form covered in suppurating sores and leaking vile, glutinous fluids from rusted tears in its bloated power armour. It carried a dripping, yellowed sword and a vile pus oozed from its face.

Even the normally unflappable instructor appeared to be repulsed by these beings and swallowed hard before continuing.

"The identity of these targets are unknown, though they have been sighted on numerous occasions in the last century on worlds surrounding Cadia. Astropathic psychometry has inferred that these individuals attempted to journey to the centre of the Eye of Terror in search of the Heart of Chaos. What that is or whether such a thing is even possible, is outside our remit, but repeated readings of the Emperor's Tarot reveals that these targets have a crucial role in the Despoiler's plans. What that role is, we do not know. That it is important to Abaddon is reason enough to prevent it coming to fruition."

The glow of the holo-slate faded as the room lights came up and the instructor stood before his team.

"After many centuries, these traitors have gathered once more under the banner of their master, and the dire portents of their return should not be underestimated. The Officio Assassinorum has trained you well. You are the best, most proficient killers in the Emperor's holy realm. To you has been entrusted this task. You will not fail. Full mission briefings will be placed in your cell cogitators. Study them carefully."

The instructor nodded towards his team.

"Exitus Acta Probat," he said, knowing he would never see any of the assassins alive again.

THE CHOSEN OF ABADDON

SPECIAL RULES

Marks of Chaos

The followers of Chaos that serve their dread masters well may receive a Mark of Chaos as a reward. There are five Marks in all: one each for Khorne, Nurgle, Tzeentch and Slaanesh as well as the Mark of Chaos Undivided. The effects of the Marks are detailed in the Books of Chaos. Marks of Chaos can be applied where specified in the army list.

- No model may have more than one Mark of Chaos.
- Members of a unit must all have the same Mark or none at all.

Veteran Skills

Ten thousand years of warfare has honed the skills of the Chaos Space Marines just as their service to Chaos has augmented their powers. No conventional Space Marine has the depth or breadth of experience that the Traitor Marines have built up and consequently there are few war skills that at least some of them have not mastered. This is reflected by the ability to assign Veteran skills to independent characters or units.

The army list entries specify which characters and units may have Veteran skills. Models with no Mark of Chaos may have any number of skills, whilst models with a Mark may only have one. All models in a unit must have the same skills, including any character they form the retinue of. Skills conferred by a list entry or which are automatic to members of a certain Legion or bearers of a particular Mark of Chaos do not count toward the maximum number of skills. No model may take a Veteran skill more than once.

If a character temporarily joins a unit and has different Veteran skills to the unit, the character may not utilise any skills the unit does not have and vice-versa. If, for example, the character has counter-attack and the unit he has joined is charged neither the character nor the unit may use the counter-attack skill to move into combat.

Chaos Psychic Powers

Those who tread the path of Chaos include many who seek a short-cut to great power. Chaos Sorcerers (note that this includes all models with the sorcerer ability) are among these.

Any model with the Sorcerer ability may take a single major psychic power and as many minor psychic powers as desired. If they possess a Familiar (see Psychic Powers and Equipment) they may take an extra major power. Abilities are used following the rules in the Warhammer 40,000 rulebook. A Sorcerer may only use a single major power in a given turn. If no major power is used, then one minor power can be used per phase. Only powers that can be used in the Assault phase can be used by a model in base to base comtact with the enemy.

Fearless Units

Any units which are described as being Fearless never have to fall back and are assumed to automatically pass any Morale or Pinning checks they are required to take, even against attacks which normally force their target to fall back with no test taken.

Daemons

Daemons are not true flesh and blood; they are formed from the substance of Chaos itself. Whilst this grants them considerable power it also means that they struggle to maintain their presence in the real universe. They need to be summoned from the Warp in order to take part in battles and, unless they are conjured onto a world where there is an adequate degree of belief in the Chaos gods, their physical forms will eventually become unstable and will discorporate, returning the Daemon to the Warp.

Chaos Icons

Chaos Space Marines march to battle under the Icons of their Gods. Summoned Daemons may only break into the real universe in proximity to a unit carrying an Icon. Icons in vehicles cannot be used to summon Daemons. If Daemons cannot materialise because there is no available Icon, continue to roll in subsequent turns.

Any unit that bears a Mark of Chaos may have a basic Icon at no additional points cost. Any Lord's retinue or independent unit of Chosen can select a special Icon from the Armoury list at the points cost indicated.

Any Chaos Space Marine model in the unit may carry its Icon, which should be shown on the model. If not carried by the unit Champion, treat Unit Icon bearers as heavy weapon troopers for casualty removal purposes.

Daemon Summoning

Apart from Daemon Princes and Nurglings, all Daemons must be summoned onto the battlefield. The Daemon units will start in reserve irrespective of whether the Reserves special rule is used in the mission being played.

Starting with the second game turn roll a D6 for each Daemonic unit at the start of the Chaos turn before placing any other newly-arrived models. If you roll equal to or greater than the number shown, the unit becomes available.

Turn	2	3	4+
D6	4+	3+	2+

When a Daemon unit becomes available place the large Ordnance blast marker in contact with a model carrying a Chaos Icon. Roll the Scatter dice; do not move the template if a 'HIT' is rolled, otherwise move it 2D6" in the direction of the arrow. The Daemons are then deployed on the area covered by the marker. Daemons will only manifest next to an Icon of Chaos Undivided or an Icon belonging to a squad with the same Mark as the Daemons themselves. Thus a unit of Bloodletters of Khorne could only appear next to an Icon-bearing unit with the Mark of Chaos Undivided or the Mark of Khorne. Once they have arrived the Daemons can move and assault as normal. When placing Daemons on the Ordnance template, models which cannot be placed on the table or more than 1" from an enemy model are destroyed.

Daemonic Instability

Daemons are summoned from the Warp and in extremis will return there. In any circumstance where a Daemon unit (not including Greater Daemons or Possessed Chaos Marines) should take a Morale check they instead take an Instability Test. This is performed exactly like a Morale check, but if it is failed the Daemons do not flee but instead suffer one wound (with no saving throw possible) for each point they failed the Instability test by. For example, a unit of Plaguebearers (Ld 8) loses a round of close combat and is outnumbered (-1 Ld modifier). They take a Morale check and roll a 9, thus suffer two wounds. Daemon units cannot be led in the normal sense, consequently they cannot be joined by independent characters and always use their own Leadership for all tests. Similarly they do not benefit from re-rolls or Fearlessness conferred by wargear, vehicle upgrades or skills. A Demagogue's rantings, for example, are unlikely to influence Daemons of the Warp.

Greater Daemons and Possession

An alternative means of remaining in the real universe requires that the Daemon takes possession of a living body.

The preparation required to summon a Greater Daemon is considerable, so if it is to be effective the ritual must be performed before battle. A single Aspiring Champion model in the army will be acting as the vessel for the Daemon (known as the Daemonvessel or sometimes Daemonhost). The exact model should be noted down before the game, there is no requirement to identify it specifically to the opponent. A Greater Daemon may only possess a model bearing the Mark of Chaos Undivided or the Mark of its own patron god. A Bloodthirster could only possess a model with the Mark of Chaos Undivided or the Mark of Khorne for example.

Until the Daemon manifests, the host will fight with the Strength characteristic of the Greater Daemon itself (note that whatever wargear the model may have, its effective Strength can never go above 10).

At the start of each turn after the first that the Daemon's Host is on the battlefield, the owning player chooses either to resist the possession or invite it. Roll a D6; if the choice was to resist then the Daemon only takes possession of the vessel on a roll of 6. If the choice was to invite possession then the Daemon possesses the vessel on a roll of 4 or more. When this occurs replace the vessel model with the Greater Daemon model. If Possession occurs while the vessel is inside a transport vehicle or bunker it is assumed the host staggers out screaming before the nightmarish transformation occurs. The Aspiring Champion replaces is treated as a casualty.

If the enemy kills the host before possession occurs, the Daemon will automatically take possession of the vessel's body at the end of the player turn in which its host is killed. Place the Daemon model on the position occupied by the late vessel, in contact with the same enemy models (if any).

The possessed flesh of a dead Chaos Space Marine will not sustain a Greater Daemon forever, so at the end of each Chaos turn that the Greater Daemon has started on the battlefield after possessing a dead host, roll a special Instability test for the Daemon using 3D6 added together. If the sum of the three dice is greater than the Daemon's unmodified Leadership it suffers the difference in wounds with no save possible. A Daemon that is lost this way is considered to be dead for victory point purposes.

Daemon Weapons

> "For seventeen long centuries have I remained in this blade, confined within these metal walls. During all of my imprisonment you are the first I have seen who is worthy to bear me into battle. Come, take my hilt, and I will serve you in the manner of my kind, drawing the blood of your enemies, protecting you in the midst of the fight, bringing you safe home again. Now draw me from the scabbard and test the fitness of my balance. See how easily I swing, how my keen edge cleaves the air. A good choice, am I not?"
>
> "Willingly you picked me up. Your first mistake. Willingly you drew me. Your second mistake. I do not allow my servants to make three mistakes, foolish mortal..."

Forged in the flames of darkest evil, Daemon swords, blades and axes are amongst the most potent of weapons. Each blade contains the bound essence of a denizen of the Warp, whose terrifying powers may be employed by a bearer strong enough to gain mastery over it. But even the strongest may be forced to pay a price, for should the blade still thirst for souls when all enemies lay slain, then it may just turn its attentions on the one who wields it.

Unique Weapons

Daemon weapons are much sought after weapons. You may only include a single Daemon Weapon in your army. Daemon weapons carried by special characters do not count towards this limit. Only weapons from the Deamon Weapons section of the armoury, or those specifically listed as such in the Books of Chaos, count as Daemon weapons.

Just because a weapon is described as a blade or sword does not mean it always takes this form. Modellers should feel free to represent a Daemon weapon how they wish, as long as it looks suitably impressive and they inform their opponents what it is.

Some Daemon weapons are two-handed. This is specified in the weapon's description. A model wielding a two-handed weapon may not use an additional close combat weapon. There is no additional strength benefit from using such a weapon beyond the normal abilities of the weapon.

The costs and rules for individual Daemon weapons can be found in the Gifts and Wargear section (on pages 14 and 19), and in the Books of Chaos (pages 46 to 65). Some Daemon weapons may only be used by a model with a particular Mark. These will be found in the relevant Book of Chaos.

Mastery

In any player turn that the bearer inflicts at least one casualty on the enemy with a Daemon weapon, the Daemon may gain enough strength to resist its owner. This battle of wills can be draining or even fatal for the wielder. Make a Leadership test at the end of the turn. If the test is failed the wielder suffers a 'Perils of the Warp' attack. If the test is passed or if the wielder survives the Daemon's attack he re-asserts his mastery and continues as normal (at least until the Daemon weapon rebels again!) Note that this is a Leadership test, not a Morale check, so characters who are Fearless must still take this test.

CHAOS SPACE MARINE ARMOURY

Marks of Chaos

All the Marks of Chaos are shown in the following table. See the Books of Chaos for more details on these.

Mark of Chaos Undivided* . . . . . .5/1 pts
Mark of Khorne* . . . . .10/5 pts
Mark of Slaanesh* . . . . .10/5 pts
Mark of Nurgle* . . . . .10/5 pts
Mark of Tzeentch* . . . . .10 pts

Weapons

One-handed Weapons

Bolt Pistol . . . . .1 pt
Chainfist (Terminators only)* . .30/18 pts
Close combat weapon* . . . . .1 pt
Lightning Claw* . . . . .25/15 pts
Plasma Pistol . . . . .15/10 pts
Power Fist* . . . . .25/15 pts
Power Weapon* . . . . .15/10 pts

Two-handed Weapons

Bolter .2 pts
Combi-bolter* . . . . .3 pts
Combi-flamer* . . . . .10/5 pts
Combi-melta* . . . . .15/10 pts
Great weapon . . . . .3 pts
Pair of Lightning Claws* . . . . . . .30 pts

Wargear

All models with access to the Armoury may select items from this list.

Bionics* . . . . .5 pts
Chaos Hound . . . . .12 pts each
Chaos Marine Bike . . . . .30/20 pts
Frag Grenades . . . . .1 pts
Krak Grenades . . . . .2 pts
Master-crafted weapon* . . . . . .15/10 pts
Melta Bombs . . . . .5 pts
Personal Icon* . . . . .10 pts
Spiky Bits* . . . . .10 pts
Teleport Homer* . . . . .5 pts
Terminator armour . . . . .25/19 pts

Psychic Abilities & Equipment

These items and abilities are only available to Sorcerers. The army list details which models can be Sorcerers.

Doombolt* . . . . .15 pts
Familiar* . . . . .5 pts
Gift of Chaos* . . . . .20 pts
Mass Mutation . . . . .25 pts
Minor Psychic Power* . . . . .10 pts
Warp Focus* . . . . .10 pts
Warp Talisman* . . . . .5 pts
Wind of Chaos* . . . . .20 pts

Daemonic Gifts

These are the gifts of the Chaos Gods. All models with access to the Armoury may select abilities from this list.

Daemon Armour . . . . .20/10 pts
Daemonic Aura . . . . .15/10 pts
Daemon Chains* . . . . .20 pts
Daemonic Essence* . . . . .15/- pts
Daemon Fire* . . . . .5 pts
Daemonic Flight . . . . .20/10 pts
Daemonic Mutation* . . . . .15/10 pts
Daemonic Resilience* . . . . .10 pts
Daemonic Rune* . . . . .35 pts
Chaos Spawn* . . . . .20 pts
Daemonic Speed . . . . .15/10 pts
Daemonic Strength* . . . . .10/5 pts
Daemonic Stature (Lord only) . . . .15 pts
Daemonic Steed . . . . .25/15 pts
Daemonic Talons . . . . .10/5 pts
Daemonic Venom . . . . .5/3 pts
Daemonic Visage* . . . . .5/2 pts

Veteran Skills

See the Special Rules for Veteran skills. These skills can be assigned to units as well as characters.

Counter-attack* . . . . .10/2 pts
Furious Charge* . . . . .15/3 pts
Infiltrate . . . . .15/3 pts
Move Through Cover . . . . .5/1 pts
Night Vision* . . . . .5/1 pts
Siege Specialists* . . . . .5/1 pts
Skilled Riders* . . . .-/2 pts
Tank Hunters* . . . . .15/3 pts

Gifts of the Gods

The items and abilities listed here are only available to models with the Mark of the Chaos god in question. They are listed here for convenience when working out your army – see the Books of Chaos for full details. All gifts except Psychic powers are considered Daemonic Gifts.

Gifts of Khorne

Axe of Khorne* . . . . .20/15 pts
Banner of Rage* . . . . .20 pts
Berserker Glaive* (Daemon weapon) 40 pts
Collar of Khorne* . . . . .5 pts
Feel no Pain* . . . . .10/5 pts
Juggernaut of Khorne . . . . .35 pts
Khornate Chainaxe . . . . .3/1 pts
Rage of Khorne . . . . .15 pts
Talisman of Burning Blood . . . . .10/5 pts

Gifts of Slaanesh

Allure of Slaanesh . . . . .25 pts
Aura of Acquiescence* . . . . .10 pts
Combat Drugs* . . . . .25 pts
Doom Siren* . . . . .10 pts
Lash of Torment* (Daemon weapon) .25 pts
Minor Psychic Power* . . . . .10 pts
Needle of Desire* (Daemon weapon) .25 pts
Rapturous Standard* . . . . .50 pts
Sonic Blaster* . . . . .5 pts
Steed of Slaanesh . . . . .25 pts

Gifts of Nurgle

Blight Grenades . . . . .25 pts
Manreaper* (Daemon Weapon) .25 pts
Minor Psychic Power* . . . . .10 pts
Nurgling Infestation* . . . . .20 pts
Nurgle's Rot* . . . . .5 pts
Pandemic Staff* (Daemon Weapon) .25 pts
Plague Sword* . . . . .25/15 pts
Plague Banner* . . . . .50 pts

Gifts of Tzeentch

Bedlam Staff* (Daemon Weapon) .25 pts
Blasted Standard* . . . . .50 pts
Bolt of Change* . . . . .30 pts
Disc of Tzeentch* . . . . .30 pts
Eye of Tzeentch* . . . . .20 pts
Inferno bolts* . . . . .10 pts
Minor Psychic Power* . . . . .10 pts
Talisman of Tzeentch* . . . . .5 pts
Thrall Wizard* . . . . .5 pts each
Twisting Path* . . . . .15 pts
Warp Blade* (Daemon Weapon) . .25 pts

Daemon Weapons

The following Daemon weapons can be used by any model irrespective of the Mark of Chaos they bear. Other examples can be found in the Books of Chaos. The cost of a Daemon weapon counts towards the total spent on Daemonic Gifts

Dark Blade* . . . . .25 pts
Dreadaxe* . . . . .25 pts
Ether Lance* . . . . .35 pts
Kai Gun* . . . . .25 pts

Chaos Vehicle Upgrades

Blasphemous Rune . . . . .10 pts
Coruscating Warp Flame (Tzeentch) 15 pts
Daemonic Possession . . . . .20 pts
Destroyer (Khorne) . . . . .25 pts
Dirge Caster . . . . .15 pts
Dozer Blade . . . . .5 pts
Extra Armour . . . . .5 pts
Havoc Launcher . . . . .25 pts
Living Vehicle . . . . .20 pts
Mutated Hull . . . . .30 pts
Parasitic Possession . . . . .20/40 pts
Pintle Combi-bolter . . . . .10 pts
Plague Carrier (Nurgle) . . . . .15 pts
Searchlight . . . . .1 pt
Smoke launcher . . . . .3 pts
Warp Amp (Slaanesh) . . . . .20 pts

Models in Terminator armour may only use items marked with a *.

Where an item has two points values, the first value is for independent characters, the second is for Aspiring Champions (or squad members if the item is a Veteran Skill). If one value is a '-' the item is not available to those models. Items with a single points value cost the same for any model allowed to purchase it.

A Chaos Lord may spend 150 points from the armoury, up to 100 points of which may be Daemonic Gifts. Other characters may spend 75 points, of which up to 50 may be Daemonic Gifts.

Kthelmir, Supplicor of Chaos Undivided, and his retinue at the Second Purging of Mephites Minoris

Points Values. Where two points values are specified, the first is the cost paid by independent characters, the second is the cost paid by Aspiring Champions (and, in the case of Veteran Skills, by squad members). These upgrades are more valuable to models with multiple wounds because they will survive to use them longer so the cost for them is higher. If, instead of a number, the second value is '-' then that ability may not be selected by Aspiring Champions.

Limits. A Chaos Lord may not have more than 150 points of wargear and Daemonic Gifts and of this total no more than 100 points can be Daemonic Gifts. Other characters are limited to 75 points of wargear and Daemonic Gifts, and of this total no more than 50 points can be Daemonic Gifts. No model may have more than one of each item of Wargear unless specifically stated in the rules for the item. Marks of Chaos and items from the weapons and Psychic abilities and equipment sections of the Armoury do not count towards the wargear points limits. With the exception of Psychic powers, all wargear and equipment in the Books of Chaos count towards the Daemonic Gifts points total.

Terminators. Only items marked with * may be used by a model in Terminator armour.

Weapons. Models may carry up to two weapons but only one may be two-handed. Note that Daemonic Gifts which function as weapons, such as the Axe of Khorne, count toward the weapon limit.

Steeds. A model may only select a single steed and may not then be transported in a vehicle. They may not use any movement mode other than that used by the mount.

Movement Modes. Daemonic Gifts may confer the ability to move as if wearing a jump pack or as if cavalry. Similarly a Chaos Space Marine Bike confers the ability to move as a bike. Refer to the relevant pages of the Warhammer 40,000 rulebook for these special movement rules. No model may have more than one of these special movement modes however they are obtained.

Followers. Some special equipment takes the form of followers who accompany the model selecting the wargear. If selected by an Independent Character these will form a unit with that character but do not prevent that character joining a unit as normal. If selected by a model that is not an independent character they will form part of the unit that the character belongs to. All followers are removed if their owner is killed.

Toughness. It is possible to improve a model's Toughness with the Mark of Nurgle or some Daemonic Gifts. The model's unmodified Toughness is the one used to determine whether an attack inflicts 'Instant Death' however. The only exception to this is the extra Toughness granted by Daemonic Stature. A model with this ability would have 5 Toughness and would not therefore be killed outright by a wound from a Strength 9 lascannon if it had more than one wound remaining.

Chainfist

A chainfist is simply a power fist fitted with an attachment designed to carve through armoured bulkheads or armoured vehicles. It is treated exactly as a power fist, but roll 2D6 for its Armour Penetration value. A chainfist may only be used by a model in Terminator armour.

Combi-bolter

Fires as a bolter but may re-roll any misses in a Shooting phase. Each miss can only be re-rolled once.

Combi-flamer

May fire either as a bolter or as a flamer. May only fire as a flamer once per game.

Combi-melta

May fire either as a bolter or as a meltagun. May only fire as a meltagun once per game.

Great weapon

A great weapon is a larger and heavier version of a close combat weapon. It is wielded in two hands thereby preventing the use of an additional close combat weapon but can be swung with more power so it adds +1 to the user's Strength in close combat.

Lightning Claws

These count as a power weapon and the model wearing them may re-roll any to wound rolls that fail to wound. Models who are armed with Lightning claws only receive the +1 Attack modifier for an additional close combat weapon if the second weapon is also another Lightning claw, as they are generally used as a pair.

Bionics

Bionics allow a Chaos Space Marine who has suffered a disabling injury or mutation to return to service. Bionic replacements will function just like the limb or organ they have replaced but there is a chance that an attack or shot will hit a bionic part and be deflected. Any wound suffered may therefore be ignored on a roll of 6. Wounds which allowed no armour save or with a Strength which is at least twice the victim's unmodified Toughness cannot be ignored as they will destroy the bionic components as easily as flesh. If the model has the 'Feel no Pain' ability then Bionics will have no effect.

Chaos Hound

Follower. The character is accompanied by up to four ferocious Chaos Hounds, each costing 12 points.

The hounds use the following profile: -

WS	BS	S	T	W	I	A	Ld	Sv
4	0	4	4	1	4	2	9	6+

Chaos Hounds move at the same speed as their Master so if he has moves 12" in the Movement phase they may move 12" in the Movement phase; if he is able to move 12" in the Assault phase they may move 12" in the Assault phase. Hounds do not have to take Difficult Terrain tests. Hounds are removed if their master is killed. Hounds may board the same transport as their master and take a single space each just as additional Chaos Space Marines would.

Chaos Space Marine Bike

Steed. Moves as Bike. Bike mounted models have +1 Toughness. Additionally, their bikes are covered in spikes granting +1 Attack. They are armed with a combi-bolter, which always counts as stationary when firing. The combi-bolter may be upgraded to a meltagun or plasma gun for +10 points or a flamer for +5 points. Chaos Space Marine Bikers get no additional benefit from the Daemonic Resilience ability, which is not cumulative with the Bike bonus. Models mounted on a Space Marine Bike gain no bonus for being armed with an additional close combat weapon, as they need one hand to control the bike.

Master-crafted weapon

This upgrade can be applied to a weapon identifying it as an especially fine and well-engineered example of its type. Apart from Daemon weapons, any close combat weapon can be master-crafted. Only ranged weapons found in the Chaos Space Marine Armoury can be master-crafted. A master-crafted close combat weapon can re-roll one miss in each round of Close Combat. A ranged weapon can re-roll one miss each Shooting phase. A miss can only be re-rolled once.

Personal Icon

The model bears a personal Icon of the Chaos Gods. The Icon will be aligned with whatever power the model bears the Mark of. The personal Icon can be used as a focus for Daemon Summoning just like unit Icons.

Spiky Bits

Chaos Space Marine armour includes many spikes, horns and blades. These are partially embellishment but can be used to deadly effect in close combat. A model equipped with spiky bits may re-roll one miss in each round of close combat. A miss can only be re-rolled once.

Teleport homer

These produce a signal that can be locked onto by teleporting troops. If the template used by teleporting troops to make a Deep Strike is centred on a model with a teleport homer then they won't scatter. Note that this only applies to teleporting troops not to troops Deep Striking because they are in drop pods, have jump packs or any other rationale. The homer must be on the table at the start of the turn it is used.

Terminator Armour

Chaos Space Marines in Terminator armour are capable of moving and firing with heavy weapons thanks to the bulky exo-skeleton and powerful servos built into the armour. They are as a result slightly cumbersome and may not be able to pursue lighter opponents so may only consolidate when victorious in close combat and may never sweeping advance. Any model in Terminator armour is capable of moving and firing with heavy weapons, has a 2+ Armour save, a 5+ Invulnerable save and adds +1 to its Attack characteristic. Terminators may teleport onto the battlefield and set up using the Deep Strike mission special rule if the mission allows these rules to be used.

DAEMONIC GIFTS

Any model that has a Daemonic Gift has started along the path to Daemonhood and only Lords close to being Daemon Princes will have several such powers. It is not possible to receive the benefit of any single Daemonic Gift twice.

Daemon Armour

The character's Chaos Space Marine armour has been blessed and sealed by the Chaos Gods and is therefore considerably more powerful. A model in Daemon armour has a 2+ armour save.

Daemonic Aura

The model has a 5+ Invulnerable saving throw, which it may use when its armour save is disregarded.

Daemon Chains

These are inscribed with powerful hexagrammic wards designed to assist in the summoning and binding of Daemons. They may only be used by a model designated to be the vessel for a Greater Daemon. When rolling for possession, the chains allow each attempt (whatever the result) to be re-rolled once.

Daemonic Essence

The model can draw vitality from the Warp, enhancing his natural reserves of power, adding +1 Wound to its profile.

Daemonic Fire

The model may project powerful warp flame from its hands, eyes or mouth. The attack is used in the Shooting phase instead of firing a weapon, using the following profile:

Range 12"   Str 4   AP 6   Assault 2

Daemon Flight

The model is able to fly using a mechanical device such as a jump pack or on mighty daemonic wings. It moves as if it has a Jump Pack (see main rulebook, page 92).

The model does not have to fly and may always choose to move as infantry in any Movement or Assault phase. Because of the bulk of its wings and/or jet packs a model with daemonic flight may not be transported aboard a vehicle.

Daemonic Mutation

The gifts of the Chaos Gods can take many ghastly forms; additional clawed limbs, barbed tails and vicious horns are commonplace. All of these mutations confer an advantage in close combat granting their bearer +1 Attack.

Daemonic Resilience

The model's body is mutated in such a way that it is especially resistant to damage. The model has +1 Toughness. This does not affect its Toughness for calculating instant death.

Daemonic Rune

The Chaos Champion has been gifted with a Daemonic Rune, a mighty symbol of the power of the Dark Gods. Their power flows through the rune demonstrating the favour conferred on the Champion. Such an individual has been marked for greatness and cannot easily be killed. Unsaved attacks whose Strength are at least double the model's Toughness will cause a single wound rather than instant death.

Daemonic Stature

The Chaos Space Marine has mutated horribly, swelling to monstrous size and taking on the aspect of a mighty Daemon Prince. The model gains +1 Strength and +1 Toughness and counts as a monstrous creature. A monstrous model ignores armour saves and rolls 2D6+ Strength for vehicle armour penetration in close combat.

The model may not ride a Steed or be transported in a vehicle. They may only wield Daemon Weapons, Axes of Khorne, Plague Swords, combi-bolters, close combat weapons or great weapons and then only if they have the appropriate Mark. Because of its huge size a model with Daemonic Stature can be shot at even if it is with a friendly unit or within 6" of one, unless it is in close combat.

The bestial power of a Chaos Lord with Daemonic Stature is best applied in close combat. Consequently his Weapon Skill is increased to 6 and his Ballistic Skill reduced to 3.

A model with Daemonic Stature is at least 10' tall (to scale!), and should always be based on a 40mm diameter base.

Daemon Steed

The model is mounted on a mutated Daemonic Steed. These steeds take many forms, more of which are described in the Books of Chaos. A typical Daemon Steed takes the form of a mighty mutated warhorse or hunting beast. It moves as Cavalry (see main rulebook, page 93) and confers the Daemonic Resilience ability upon its rider.

Daemon Spawn

Follower. The model is accompanied by a loathsome Chaos Spawn. This could be a former comrade whose original form and sanity has been lost beneath the overly generous gifts of the Chaos Gods or a victim cruelly mutated in the Eye of Terror and kept as a bound pet. The Spawn has the following profile:

WS	BS	S	T	W	I	A	Ld	Sv
3	0	5	5	2	3	D6	9	3+

Spawn move as infantry and may not be transported in vehicles. If their master is killed, the Spawn is also removed. A model accompanied by a Spawn may not Infiltrate.

Daemonic Speed

The model has mutations such as long limbs or four legs which allow it to move as Cavalry (see main rulebook, page 93).

The model does not have to move at full speed and may always choose to move as infantry in any Movement or Assault phase. If it disembarks from a vehicle in its Movement phase then it can only move as infantry in the subsequent Assault phase.

Daemonic Strength

The model has inhuman physical power such that it can snap the spine of a normal man with ease. The model has +1 Strength.

Daemonic Talons

The model has unnaturally sharp talons and horns. It may use no other weapons but will always count as having an additional close combat weapon. Any rolls to hit of 6 will inflict an automatic wound with no armour save possible.

If a creature with Daemonic Talons rolls a 6 for its Armour Penetration dice roll against a vehicle, it rolls another D6 and adds the result to the total Armour Penetration score.

Daemon Venom

The model has been gifted with a mutation that makes its attacks venomous. The model may have no other weapons but counts as having a pair of close combat weapons representing raking claws and fangs. When rolling to wound the model will never require more than 4+ irrespective of relative Strength and Toughness.

Daemonic Visage

The model is terrifying to look upon and fills his enemies with preternatural dread. If a unit has to take a Morale check after losing a close combat and the enemy includes models with Daemonic Visage the morale test is at -1 Leadership. If all of a unit's opponents have the ability, or one of them is a Greater Daemon then the test is at -2 Leadership instead.

SPECIAL ICONS

Daemon Icon

May only be carried by a unit of Chosen bearing the Mark of Chaos Undivided. A Daemon Icon is a Chaos Undivided Icon which, as well as acting as a focus for summoning Daemons normally, is a powerful conjuration and binding tool as well. At the start of the game a single nominated Daemon unit may be enslaved within the Icon. At the start of the Chaos player's turn this unit can be automatically summoned without making a Reserves roll. The Daemons will not scatter and the template is placed in contact with the Icon. The unit can move in the Movement phase and assault as normal.

Icon of Chaos Undivided

May only be carried by a unit of Chosen bearing the Mark of Chaos Undivided. A Chaos Icon is a powerful focus for the energies of Chaos Undivided. It can be used to summon Daemons onto the battlefield as normal and in addition any unit or model bearing the Mark of Chaos Undivided with a model within 6" of the Icon becomes Fearless.

PSYCHIC ABILITIES AND EQUIPMENT

Doombolt

Doombolt is a psychic power that may be used in the model's Shooting phase instead of using another ranged weapon. A Psychic test must be passed in order to use the power. When used, Doom Bolt counts as a weapon with the following profile. Roll to hit and wound as normal.

Range 18"   Str 5   AP 4   Assault 3

Familiar

A Sorcerer can normally only have one major psychic power, but a Sorcerer with a Daemonic Familiar may have two. Only one major power may be used per player turn though. The Familiar is always assumed to be on the same base as its master, although it is permissible to represent it separately for modelling purposes. It does not count as an extra model, takes up no space in transport vehicles and is only removed when its master is removed.

Gift of Chaos

A Chaos Sorcerer may use this psychic power in the Shooting phase instead of shooting. The Sorcerer may be in close combat at the time as may the target. Pick an enemy model or a friendly model within 2" of the Sorcerer and then take a Psychic test in order to use the power. If the test is successful, roll a D6. If you roll over the victim's Toughness (use the base Toughness, not the modified Toughness for being on a bike for example), or you roll a 6 no matter what the victim's Toughness is, then the victim is transformed into a Chaos Spawn, with no armour save allowed (invulnerable saves may be taken as normal). If no Chaos Spawn model is available to replace the model transformed then just remove it as a casualty.

See the Wargear section for the Chaos Spawn profile. The new Chaos Spawn will form a unit with the Sorcerer who transformed him. They are counted as being part of the Chaos army from the moment they are transformed and may attack in that Assault phase, as long as they have not already done so. Models turned into Chaos Spawn are treated as having been killed for Victory point purposes, even if the Spawn survives the battle. The only friendly models that may be transformed are Chaos Space Marines (of any type), not followers.

Mass Mutation

This psychic power can be used in the Shooting phase instead of shooting. It can only be used if the Sorcerer is currently either part of or has joined a unit of Chosen, Possessed Chaos Space Marines, Chaos Space Marines or Chaos Havocs. Provided that the Sorcerer makes a successful Psychic test, he power of Chaos warps and transforms the unit as Daemons rush from the Warp to temporarily inhabit the bodies of the Chaos Space Marines. The effect lasts until the start of the next Chaos turn even if the psyker is killed. The unit gains one ability determined at random from the list below. Remember that the benefits of a single Daemonic ability are not cumulative. Followers attached to the affected unit cannot be transformed as they are not worthy of such gifts.

1. No benefit. The unit morphs and changes but no useful mutation emerges. Roll a D6 for each member of the unit; on a roll of 1 the model is transformed into a mewling, helpless spawn and is removed as a casualty.

2. Unit gains Daemonic Strength

3. Unit gains Daemonic Visage

4. Unit gains Daemonic Resilience

5. Unit gains Daemonic Aura

6. Unit gains Daemonic Mutation

Minor Psychic Power

Sorcerers may use the general Minor Psychic Powers detailed in Chapter Approved in White Dwarf 258 and in the Chapter Approved Annual 2003 if these optional rules are being used. See Chaos Psychic Powers special rule.

Sorcerer

A character with this skill is able to use psychic powers. The skill is not available to any model with a Mark of Khorne. See Chaos Psychic Powers special rule.

Warp Focus

This is a weapon upgrade that can be conferred on any close combat weapon including Daemon weapons. The Weapon is inscribed with runes of arcane power that allow the Sorcerer to channel his powers through it. The Focus adds D6" to the range of any psychic power projected through it except Wind of Chaos. Roll for additional range each time a power is used.

Warp Talisman

A Warp Talisman demonstrates that the bearer is favoured by the Chaos Gods. It allows a Sorcerer to re-roll a Psychic test. This ability may only be used once per battle.

Wind of Chaos

This is a psychic power that may be used in the model's Shooting phase instead of firing another weapon. It takes different forms depending on the Sorcerer casting it. Worshippers of Nurgle project a stream of bilious, acidic slime that burns and infects the target. Sorcerers of Slaanesh create a golden cloud that sets every nerve end alight with rapturous agony. A Psychic test must be passed in order to use the power. Place the flamer template so that its narrow end is touching the model using this power. Any models fully or partially under the template suffer one wound on a D6 roll of 4+, with no armour or cover saves allowed (Invulnerable saves may be taken as normal). Models without a Toughness characteristic are unaffected.

VETERAN ABILITIES

Counter-Attack

Unengaged veterans in a unit that has been assaulted may move up to 6" to get into base-to-base contact with the enemy. Treat the counter-attack as an assault move, so take terrain into account as normal.

Models that counter-attack do not receive the +1 attack bonus for charging but will be able to fight with their full complement of attacks. Models may counter-attack if the unit they are in was charged as part of a 'sweeping advance', in which case the move is made immediately after the unit that made the sweeping advance completes its move.

Furious Charge

During an Assault phase in which the unit charges, all models will be at +1 Initiative and +1 Strength.

Infiltrate

The squad may deploy using the Infiltrators scenario special rule, if allowed to do so by the mission being played. Models with a bike, a Steed, Followers, Daemonic Stature, the Mark of Khorne or Terminator Armour cannot use this skill.

Move Through Cover

The squad rolls an extra D6 when rolling to move through difficult terrain. In most circumstances this will mean that they roll 3D6 and pick the dice with the highest score. Models with a Bike, a Steed, Daemonic Stature, the Mark of Khorne or Terminator Armour cannot use this skill.

Night Vision

Within the Eye of Terror there are worlds wrapped in perpetual night and worlds with underground labyrinths that stretch forever. Chaos Marines accustomed to such places develop a sixth sense more efficient than any mere technology to enable them to master the night. When the Night Fight mission special rules are in use, Veterans with Night Vision may re-roll the dice when rolling to determine how far they can see but must abide by the re-roll even if it is worse.

Siege Specialists

The unit gets +1 on any Armour Penetration rolls against enemy bunkers and tank traps. When crossing minefields they will only trigger a mine on a roll of 6.

When occupying fortifications in missions where they are the defenders, these Veterans are treated as being Fearless

They may never use the Voluntary Fall Back optional rule but test for Pinning as normal. Outside fortifications, and in fortifications built by the enemy (ie, when attacking) they get no benefit.

Skilled Riders

Only available to units mounted on Chaos Space Marine Bikes or Daemonic Beasts. The unit re-rolls any 1s rolled for Difficult Terrain tests but must accept the new result. Remember that all independent characters have this ability, so do not need to pay points for it.

Tank Hunters

The unit always passes any Morale checks due to tank shock and adds +1 to all Armour Penetration rolls made with heavy weapons, special weapons, melta-bombs and krak grenades.

DAEMON WEAPONS

Dark Blade

The Dark Blade is jet-black, no reflection or mark mars the perfect satin darkness of its blade although the hilt, pommel and grip are often richly embellished. The Dark Blade is a hungry killer that feasts on the souls of the slain and urges its bearer on to further acts of barbarity until it is sated.

A Dark Blade is a power weapon that adds +2 to its bearer's Strength when resolving to wound rolls or Armour Penetration rolls.

Dreadaxe

The Dreadaxe contains an entrapped entity with a vampiric thirst for souls that is especially partial to destroying daemonic rivals. This blade is death to all who oppose its bearer.

No hits made with the Dreadaxe will ever need have a To Wound roll of worse than 4+ regardless of relative Strength and Toughness values. Wounds from the Dreadaxe ignore invulnerable saving throws (but not armour saving throws). It has no special abilities against vehicles.

Ether Lance

The Ether Lance is a conduit to the Warp. Its bearer can launch bolts of Empyrean energy at his foes or draw them into the lance, eventually consuming them utterly.

The Ether Lance is a power weapon. In the Shooting phase it may fire with the following profile.

Range: Template Str 4 AP 3 Assault 1

Kai Gun

When warp storm Gae-sann enveloped the Kai system in M34 it absorbed into the Eye of Terror a powerful industrial culture. The Machine Smiths of Kai bartered their skills for a measure of protection, learning to fashion weapons in the Warp that they could not have conceived before. Their ploy eventually failed and the Daemon hordes descended to fight for the possession of these new domains. All that remained after the destruction of Kai was the weapons they had built to appease their slayers.

The Kai Gun is a huge bolter of archaic design, so large that a normal man would be unable to lift it. It is a two-handed weapon. The gun is a psychic catalyst, turning the hate and malice of its firer into tangible bolts of energy. The Kai Gun is used as a normal ranged weapon with the following profile:

Range: 24" Str 6 AP 3 Assault 2

VEHICLE UPGRADES

Blasphemous Rune

The hull of the vehicle is daubed with the symbols of the Chaos Gods. These blasphemous scrawls are disturbing and can unnerve the most experienced troops. Enemy tank shocked by the vehicle subtract -1 from their Leadership. If scribed on a Dreadnought any Morale checks taken by enemy in close combat with it are at -1.

Daemonic possession

This upgrade cannot be chosen for open-topped vehicles. The vehicle does not have any crew, instead it is possessed by a Daemon. Hatches are all welded shut and sealed with runes and sigils. The vehicle may no longer transport any troops. The Daemon controls the vehicle and may ignore 'shaken' and 'stunned' results. A vehicle may be subject to both parasitic possession and daemonic possession.

Dirge caster

The Dirge Caster is a broadcaster, which outputs a non-stop litany of Chaos. Incomprehensible and disturbing to all others, the sound enthrals and absorbs the followers of Chaos, driving out any uncertainty or doubt. Apart from Daemons, all Chaos units with a model within 6" of a vehicle with a Dirge Caster become Fearless (see Special Rules on page 12). A Dirge Caster cannot be mounted on a vehicle with a Warp Amp (see Book of Slaanesh).

Dozer Blade

Vehicles equipped with dozer blades may re-roll a failed Difficult Terrain test as long as they are not moving more than 6" that turn. May not be fitted to Dreadnoughts or Defilers.

Extra Armour

This represents additional armour added by the vehicle's crew. Vehicles so equipped count 'crew stunned' results as 'crew shaken' results instead.

Havoc Launcher

The Havoc launcher is a multiple missile launcher commonly mounted on Chaos vehicles. Its profile is as follows.

Range 48" Str 4 AP 6 Heavy2/Blast

If two hits are scored on a unit place the blast marker once to determine the number of models that are hit and double the result after rolling for partial hits.

Living Vehicle

The vehicle is able to attack like a living creature using blades, tentacles, lashes or spurts of flame and bile. In the Shooting phase it may attack any enemy unit within 3" with D6 BS4 S4 Ap - attacks. This attack can be made in addition to any normal shooting attacks, but only if the vehicle could normally make at least one Shooting attack. Units attacked do not count as being in close combat and can move freely in their next Movement phase.

A 'Weapon Destroyed' result against a living vehicle may choose to eliminate its close combat weapons. Immobilised results have no effect on its ability to make close combat attacks.

Mutated hull

The vehicle's hull has been changed by the Dark Gods. Set with spikes, gargoyles and arcane symbols the hull writhes and reforms each time it is hit. The armour value of each of the vehicle's locations is increased by +1 point, up to a maximum of 14.

Parasitic Possession

The vehicle has been possessed by a parasitic daemon that infests the hull. The Daemon eats into the construction and insinuates itself into every part of the vehicle. Whilst appearing ramshackle as a consequence the vehicle is held together by the Daemon. At the end of the Chaos player's turn any 'Immobilised' or 'Weapon Destroyed' effects are repaired on a roll of 4+.

Use the lower points cost for vehicle whose base cost (including weapons but excluding vehicle upgrades) is less than 150, the higher points cost for a vehicle that costs 150 points or more.

Pintle Combi-bolter

The combi-bolter is the standard additional pintle armament for Chaos Space Marine vehicles. They are treated as an extra twin-linked bolter that may be used in addition to any other weapons the vehicle can fire. it may not be fired if the vehicle moves more than 6". The combi-bolter can be upgraded to either a combi-flamer or a combi-melta at +5 pts. May not be fitted to Dreadnoughts or Defilers. No more than one pintle combi-bolter vehicle upgrade can be fitted to any vehicle.

Searchlight

Searchlights are only of use in missions using the Night Fighting special rule. Searchlights allow one enemy unit spotted by the vehicle to be fired at by any other friendly units that are in range and have a line of fire, without them having to determine how far they can see first. A vehicle that uses its searchlight in this way is similarly exposed and can be fired on by any enemy units that are in range and have a line of fire in their turn.

Smoke launcher

See the rules for smoke launchers on page 88 of the Warhammer 40,000 rulebook.

CHAOS SPACE MARINES ARMY LIST

This section of the book is given over to the Chaos Space Marine army list, a listing of the different troops and vehicles a Chaos Lord can use in battle or, in your case, games of Warhammer 40,000. The army list allows you to fight battles using the scenarios included in the Warhammer 40,000 rulebook, but it also provides you with the basic information you'll require to field a Chaos Space Marine army in scenarios you've devised yourself, as part of a campaign series of games, or whatever else may take your fancy.

The army list is split into five sections. All of the squads, vehicles and characters in an army list are placed in one of the five sections depending upon their role on the battlefield. In addition every model included in the army list is given a points value, which varies depending upon how effective that model is on the battlefield.

Before you can choose an army for a game you will need to agree with your opponent upon a scenario and upon the total number of points each of you will spend on your army. Having done this you can proceed to pick an army as described below.

USING A FORCE ORGANISATION CHART

The army lists are used in conjunction with the force organisation chart from a scenario. Each force organisation chart is split into five categories that correspond to the relevant sections in the army list, and each category has one or more boxes. Each box indicates that you **may** make one choice from that section of the army list, while a dark toned box means that you **must** make a choice from that section.

USING THE ARMY LISTS

To make a choice, look in the relevant section in the army list and decide what unit you wish to have in your army, how many models there will be in the unit, and which upgrades that you want (if any). Remember that you cannot field models that are equipped with weapons and wargear not shown on the model. Once this is done subtract the points value of the unit from your total points, and then go back and make another choice. Continue doing this until you have spent all your points. Now you are ready to crush the weakling Imperium of Man!

Army List entries

Each army list entry consists of the following:

Unit Name: The type of unit, which may also show a limitation on the minimum or maximum number of choices you can make of that unit type (0-1, for example).

Profile: These are the characteristics of that unit type, including its points cost. Where the unit has different warriors, there may be more than one profile. Where two saving throws are shown, the one before the slash is an armour save and the one after is an invulnerable save.

Number/Squad: This shows the number of models in the unit, or the number of models you may take for one choice from the Force Organisation chart. Often this is a variable amount, in which case it shows the minimum and maximum unit size.

Weapons: These are the unit's standard weapons.

Options: This lists the different weapon and equipment options for the unit and any additional points cost for taking these options. If a squad is allowed to have models with upgrades, then these must be given to ordinary team members, not the character.

Special Rules: This is where you'll find any special rules that apply to the unit.

STANDARD MISSIONS

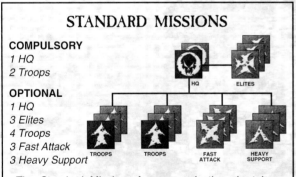

COMPULSORY
1 HQ
2 Troops

OPTIONAL
1 HQ
3 Elites
4 Troops
3 Fast Attack
3 Heavy Support

The Standard Missions force organisation chart is a good example of how to choose an army.

To begin with you will need at least one HQ unit and two Troops units (dark shaded boxes indicate units that must be taken for the mission).

This leaves the following for you to choose from to make up your army's total points value:

Up to 1 additional HQ unit,

0-3 additional Elite units,

0-4 additional Troops units,

0-3 additional Fast Attack units,

0-3 additional Heavy Support units.

Chaos Lords are the most powerful of the Chaos Space Marines. With the genetic advantages of a Space Marine, millennia of combat experience and the blessings of the Dark Gods there are few more dangerous entities in the Galaxy. Chaos Lords are warriors who have within them the will, skill and strength to be the greatest of Mankind's heroes. Their tragedy is that they have chosen to be Mankind's greatest nemesis.

At the right hand of many a Chaos Lord stands a trusted lieutenant. These are powerful fighters in their own right and may aspire to leadership should anything 'unfortunate' happen to their master.

0-1 Chaos Lord or Chaos Sorcerer Lord or Daemon Prince

	Pts/Model	WS	BS	S	T	W	I	A	Ld	Sv
Chaos Lord	60	5	5	4	4	3	5	3	10	3+

Number/squad: 1

Weapons: The Chaos Lord selects equipment from the Chaos Armoury.

Options: A Chaos Lord may have a single Mark of Chaos and has access to the Chaos Armoury and the Veteran Skill list.

A Lord may be upgraded to a Sorcerer Lord for +10 points. This allows him to select from the Psychic Abilities and Equipment section of the Chaos Armoury.

Chaos Lord is the term used to describe a commander who is still largely a Space Marine; the more Daemonic gifts he has the further he has progressed towards being a Daemon Prince. As a guideline a Chaos Lord with more than 50 points of daemonic abilities can claim to be a Daemon Prince and should be modelled appropriately.

Character: The Chaos Lord is an independent character and follows all the independent character special rules as given in the Warhammer 40,000 rulebook. If accompanied by a retinue he must stay in unit coherency with it while any members remain.

SPECIAL RULES
Retinue: The Chaos Lord may be accompanied by a Retinue of Chosen (see the Chosen entry on page 24 for further details).

> *"Twelve times has the Despoiler held the galaxy within his grasp, and each time he had but to claim what was his for the taking. I am now sure there exists some greater scheme, some unfathomable logic driving Abaddon in his endeavours. I ask myself, 'Why has he not claimed the gifts the ruinous powers must certainly have proffered him? Why does he still walk amongst mortals when surely the path of elevation to Daemonhood has been set before him twelve times and more?' The one conclusion I can draw is that the Despoiler's motives lie not with the abstract, spiritual power of the Empyrean: more, they lie with the mundane, with physical, earthly power. Abaddon is driven by hatred and bitterness, to such an extent that he will not rest until he sees righted the wrong he perceives committed against him and his kind ten millennia past by our lord the Emperor. Perhaps after his thirteenth Black Crusade he will consider his mission complete, and only then will he assume the mantle of Daemonhood, over the very ashes of the Imperium."*
>
> *The Heretic Archivist of the Gethsemane Reclusium (executed 963.M41)*

Chaos Lieutenant or Chaos Sorcerer

	Pts/Model	WS	BS	S	T	W	I	A	Ld	Sv
Chaos Lieutenant	45	5	5	4	4	2	5	3	10	3+

Number/squad: 1

Weapons: The Chaos Champion selects equipment from the Chaos Armoury.

Options: A Chaos Lieutenant may have a single Mark of Chaos and has access to the Chaos Armoury and the Veteran Skill list.

A Lieutenant may be upgraded to a Sorcerer for +10 points. This allows him to select from the Psychic Abilities and Equipment section of the Chaos Armoury.

Character: The Chaos Lieutenant is an independent character and follows all the Independent Character special rules as given in the Warhammer 40,000 rulebook. If accompanied by a retinue he must stay in unit coherency with it while any members remain.

SPECIAL RULES
Retinue: The Chaos Lieutenant may be accompanied by a Retinue of Chosen (see the Chosen for further details)

0-1 Greater Daemon

	Pts/Model	WS	BS	S	T	W	I	A	Ld	Sv
Bloodthirster	205	9	0	8	6	4	4	5	10	3+/4+
Great Unclean One	150	5	3	7	6	6	2	3	10	-/4+
Lord of Change	160	8	4	6	6	4	6	3	10	-/4+
Keeper of Secrets	160	7	3	7	6	4	4	5	10	-/4+

Number/squad: 1

Weapons: Although they may carry weapons, the effectiveness of Greater Daemons is exactly as shown on the profile above.

Options: Greater Daemons may not select from the Chaos Armoury except for Major and Minor psychic powers. See the Sorcerer special rule for more details.

Character: Each Greater Daemon is an independent character and follows all the Independent Character special rules as given in the Warhammer 40,000 rulebook except those relating to being shot at. Because of their sheer size it is always possible to fire at a Greater Daemon even if it has joined a unit or is within 6" of another viable target.

Transport: A Greater Daemon may not ride in a transport vehicle.

SPECIAL RULES

Possession: A Greater Daemon must possess another model to enter the battlefield. See the Daemon special rules for more details.

Fearsome: Greater Daemons have the Daemonic Visage Daemonic Ability.

Fearless: Greater Daemons never take Morale checks, never fall back and cannot be pinned.

Monstrous Creature: Greater Daemons are huge and powerful opponents. They roll 2D6 for Armour Penetration and ignore their opponents' armour saves in close combat.

Invulnerable: Greater Daemons are unnatural creatures, made from the very stuff of Chaos itself and are therefore very difficult to destroy. They may therefore make an Invulnerable save against all wounds they take, even those that would normally permit no Armour save.

Bloodthirsters are martial daemons clad in the brass armour of Khorne. They, of all the Greater Daemons, receive a 3+ armour save as well as a 4+ Invulnerable save and may choose which to use against any attack.

Daemonic Gifts. A Keeper of Secrets has the Warp Scream ability (see Book of Slaanesh). A Great Unclean One has the Nurgling Infestation and Nurgle's Rot abilities (see Book of Nurgle). The Bloodthirster and the Lord of Change have wings. This allows them to move as if they had the Daemonic Flight ability. Because of their strength and power, a winged Greater Daemon does not have to take a test if it lands in difficult terrain.

Sorcerers. All Greater Daemons, except the Bloodthirster, have psychic powers. Each may select any one psychic power from the Chaos Armoury at no cost. They may have additional Minor Psychic Abilities at the normal points cost.

- A Lord of Change may select a power available to sorcerers with the Mark of Tzeentch, and does not have to pass a Psychic test to use a psychic power.

- A Great Unclean One may select a power available to sorcerers with the Mark of Nurgle.

- A Keeper of Secrets may select a power available to sorcerers with the Mark of Slaanesh.

Living Icons: Greater Daemons are all aligned with one of the Chaos Gods; Bloodthirsters serve Khorne, Great Unclean Ones serve Nurgle, Keepers of Secrets serve Slaanesh and Lords of Change serve Tzeentch. Such is the power of Greater Daemons that each counts as an Icon of the deity they serve so lesser Daemons can be summoned adjacent to them.

Khornate Frenzy: A Bloodthirster must always assault and perform a sweeping advance whenever possible.

BLOODTHIRSTER

Of all those who shed blood in the name of Khorne, the Bloodthirster is the most terrifying, the most proficient and the most utterly savage. Wearing archaic armour forged at the base of the Blood God's throne and bearing a whip of hell-fire and an axe larger than a man, the Bloodthirster throws itself into battle upon wings that block out the light of the sun. None save the Primarchs of old were truly its equal in power.

GREAT UNCLEAN ONE

Wreathed in swarms of giggling Nurglings, the Great Unclean One shambles across the battlefield spreading disease and pestilence wherever it passes. To the mortal eye it is the foulest of servants of the Ruinous Powers, appearing as a malformed being of weeping pustules and exposed, diseased organs; few men have the stomach, let alone the ability to oppose such a being.

LORD OF CHANGE

To face a Lord of Change in battle is to stand against a master of fate itself. It unravels and deciphers what will come to pass, and uses the knowledge to confound its enemies' plans. The ultimate master of the medium of the Warp, the Lord of Change is second only to Tzeentch itself in mystic power. It's appearance reflects its capricious nature; the Lord of Change is a bizarre creature of multihued skin, massive feathered pinions and a bird-like face with eyes that shine with the ruinous light of the very depths of the Warp.

KEEPER OF SECRETS

To look upon a Keeper of Secrets is to surrender every last shred of self-will. It knows the most secret desires of every mortal being, and will use this horrific knowledge to gain power over its foes, seducing them with promises none can resist. But the Keeper of Secrets is not just a master of the psyche; on the field of battle it is a lithe and dextrous killer, gifting all with the most delicate of killing strokes and the most deadly of caresses.

ELITES

The Chosen are the elite of a Chaos Space Marine army. Drawn from the most experienced and capable warriors of the Traitor Legions, they have literally thousands of years of experience. These men have ruled planets, led armies and destroyed civilisations; they are the Chosen of the Chaos gods and the bane of all that lives.

Chosen

	Pts/Model	WS	BS	S	T	W	I	A	Ld	Sv
Chosen	17	4	4	4	4	1	4	1	10	3+
Chosen Terminator	+19	4	4	4	4	1	4	2	10	2+
Chosen Aspiring Champion	+10	4	4	4	4	1	4	2	10	3+
Chosen Terminator Champion	+29	4	4	4	4	1	4	3	10	2+

Number/squad: The maximum number of Chosen that can be fielded is determined by the points limit of the game being played.

Up to 1,000 points – maximum of 10 Chosen;

1,001-2,000 points – maximum of 20 Chosen;

2,001-3,000 points – maximum of 30 Chosen;

3,001 points or more – maximum of 40 Chosen.

However many Chosen are included in the army they occupy a single Elites choice in the force organisation chart.

From 4 to 19 Chosen can be used to form retinues for the Chaos Lord and/or his Lieutenant. Additionally, a single unit of between 5 and 20 Chosen can be fielded as a normal Elites choice. Obviously these unit sizes are constrained by the maximum number of Chosen allowed for the size of army.

Character: Chosen in power armour or Terminator armour can further be upgraded to Aspiring Champions at +10 points each. Chosen Aspiring Champions have access to the Chaos Armoury, but may not choose ranged weapon upgrades from the list opposite.

Up to one Aspiring Champion in each unit or retinue can be further upgraded to a Sorcerer at +5 points.

Weapons: Each Chosen will be armed with a close combat weapon and either a bolter or a bolt pistol.

Options: Any number of Chosen in Power Armour can be upgraded to Terminators at +19 points each. Any model upgraded in this way will replace his normal weapons with a power weapon and combi-bolter. The power weapon may be upgraded to a Power Fist for +5 pts, a lightning claw for +5 pts or a chainfist for +8pts. The combi-bolter may be upgraded to a combi-flamer for +5 pts or a combi-melta for +10 pts.

Every third Chosen model in Terminator Armour in each unit or retinue may exchange their combi-bolter for a weapon from the following list:

- Upgrade combi-bolter to reaper autocannon at +20 pts
- Upgrade combi-bolter to heavy flamer at +15 pts

Chosen in power armour may have frag grenades at +1 pt and/or krak grenades at +2 pts

Every third Chosen model in power armour in each unit or retinue may exchange their bolter for a weapon chosen from the following list.

- Upgrade bolter to flamer at +6 pts
- Upgrade bolter to meltagun, plasma pistol or plasma gun at +10 pts
- Upgrade bolter to heavy bolter at +15 pts
- Upgrade bolter to missile launcher or autocannon at +20 pts
- Upgrade bolter to lascannon at +35 points

Note that a Chosen bearing a Mark of Chaos other than that of Chaos Undivided may have different weapon options. Refer to the appropriate Book of Chaos for further details.

Each Chosen unit may bear a Mark of Chaos and have Veteran skills.

Special Icon: A unit or retinue of Chosen with the Mark of Chaos Undivided may select a special Icon at a cost of +20 pts. There are two types, the Icon of Chaos Undivided and the Daemon Icon. Units with other Marks may carry a Special Icon of the Chaos God they serve. See the Books of Chaos for more details.

Transport: Each Retinue or Unit of Chosen may have a transport vehicle. If the total unit numbers ten models or less, and none have Terminator armour, they may be mounted aboard a Rhino. If any are wearing Terminator armour, total the models in the retinue, counting Terminators as two models. If there are ten model equivalents or less in total they may be mounted in a Land Raider.

Transport: Chaos Rhino

	Points	Front Armour	Side Armour	Rear Armour	BS
Chaos Rhino	50	11	11	10	4

Type: Tank   **Crew:** Chaos Space Marines

Weapons: The Chaos Rhino is armed with a combi-bolter

Options: The Chaos Rhino may be equipped with any of the vehicle upgrades allowed from the Chaos Space Marine Armoury.

Transport: The Chaos Rhino can carry up to ten Chaos Space Marines. Note that it cannot transport Terminators, Obliterators, Raptors, Daemons or Models with Daemonic Stature.

Fire Points - 1: The Rhino has a large hatch in its hull roof which can be used by up to two passengers as a fire point. This does not leave the Rhino open-topped as its passengers wear power armour.

Access Points - 3: The Rhino has two side hatches and a rear ramp, any of which can be used as access points by the passengers.

Notes: The Rhino is the most ubiquitous vehicle in the Chaos Space Marine arsenal and is renowned for its reliability and ease of maintenance. If a Rhino is immobilised and spends a Chaos turn without firing any weapons its driver may be able to effect a temporary repair that turn. Roll a D6; on a 6 the Rhino will be free to move in its next Movement phase. The check is made in the Shooting phase.

Motivated by either a deep devotion to their infernal masters or an unquenchable lust for power some Chaos Space Marines allow themselves to be possessed by Chaos Daemons. Each pact is different but Chaos Space Marines never entirely give up their self-will and normally remain the master in the blasphemous symbiotic relationship. When the stench of blood is in the air though the Daemon within them is far more powerful and the Possessed become even more bestial.

Possessed Chaos Space Marines

	Pts/Model	WS	BS	S	T	W	I	A	Ld	Sv
Possessed	22	4	4	5	4	1	4	1	10	3/5+
Possessed Aspiring Champion	+15	4	4	5	4	1	4	2	10	3/5+

Number/squad: 5-10

Weapons: Bolt pistol and close combat weapon.

Options: Possessed Chaos Space Marines have Daemonic Aura and Daemonic Strength. These have been included in their profile.

A Possessed Chaos Space Marine unit may be given a Mark of Chaos (see special rules) but may not have any Veteran skills.

A squad of Possessed Chaos Space Marines may all be upgraded with a single Daemonic Ability chosen from the following list at the cost indicated.

 Daemonic Flight at +15 pts per model
 Daemonic Talons at +5 pts per model
 Daemon Fire at +5 pts per model
 Daemonic Visage at +2 pts per model
 Daemonic Mutation at + 10 pts per model

Character: The squad may be led by an Aspiring Champion at +15 pts. The Aspiring Champion has access to the Chaos Armoury.

Transport: If the squad numbers ten Possessed Chaos Space Marines or less then it may be mounted in a Rhino at an additional cost of +50 points (see Rhino transport entry for more details) but not if any of its members have the Daemonic Flight ability.

Appendices to Report of the Scribe Historicus

Part the Seventh: Organisation of the Chaos Fleets

When Horus rebelled against the Emperor his Legions could each call upon a great armada of ships. This was the way of the times; the Primarchs were the Emperor's most trusted Lieutenants, they were the terrible young Princes of the Emperor's armies and all other men were subordinated to them. Thus when they joined Horus they brought much more than their battle-brothers, they brought war fleets so huge that they could transport the Legions and countless millions of their minions to Terra to confront the Emperor. With victory hard-won, the new masters of the Imperium would never let any individuals hold such power again. The great Legions were reduced to Chapters, a mere thousand Space Marines, with specialist ships to carry their fighting strength swiftly to battle and no more. Instead the Imperial Navy was expanded enormously; disciplined and with deeply rooted traditions its loyalties were solely to the Golden Throne.

The Traitor Legions never made such a change. Instead the ships that fled with them to the Eye of Terror remained theirs, ensuring that the Forces of Chaos are still organised around the Traitor Legions to the present day.

Their ships are often captained by non-Space Marines, many of them former privateers or rogue traders such as Abraham Thurst and Maleficia Arkham. The services of such men are so valuable to the Chaos Legions that they are assigned Chaos Marines as ship's troops and act as Fleetmasters for the greatest of the Warmasters. Such service is not without risk, as failure is not readily tolerated by the Lords of Chaos.

The total strength of the Chaos warfleets cannot be calculated – ships believed to have been lost in the Warp may appear centuries later in the service of the Chaos Space Marines. Some ships turn renegade, corrupted by the subtle machinations of Chaos Gods. Other vessels are built either within the Eye of Terror or at rogue planets in the Segmentum Obscuras. The Gothic War gave no more than an indication of the total strength of the Chaos Fleets, representing those owing allegiance to Abaddon alone. In total the Imperial Navy is certainly larger but it is spread across the galaxy whereas the enemy can concentrate their strength in the Eye of Terror before hurling themselves at the Cadian Gate. There are other ways out of the Eye but it is extremely difficult to get a large fleet through without detection or risk of loss. Prior to the start of the Gothic War, three years of carefully planned raids were needed to silence enough Imperial monitoring stations to make Abaddon's feints believable even before the main attack was launched. Whilst the Cadian Gate is strongly held major Chaos incursions are unlikely but the Imperium should always remember the calibre of the Chaos Captains before considering itself safe.

Athrix Heremongh,
by order of Inquisitor Horst

0-I Obliterator Cult

	Pts/Model	WS	BS	S	T	W	I	A	Ld	Sv
Obliterator	70	4	4	5	4(5)	2	4	2	9	2/5+

Number/squad: 1-3

Weapons: Body Weapons. For details of Obliterator weapons see below. Whilst Obliterators can be armed with more than one close combat weapon they do not receive an extra attack as this has already been included in their profile.

SPECIAL RULES

Fearless: Obliterators cannot be pinned. They are assumed to automatically pass any Morale checks they are required to take.

Body Weapons: Obliterators are able to reshape their bodies to fabricate a wide variety of weapons. Obliterators may only fire one weapon in any Shooting phase and each model may fire a different weapon from those available.

Obliterator Weapons: lascannon, autocannon, missile launcher (frag only), heavy bolter, twin-linked plasma gun, twin-linked meltagun, flamer, power fist.

Obliterators can use different weapons in different phases so they may shoot with twin-linked plasma guns and then assault using power fists.

Deep Strike: Obliterators may teleport into battle. To represent this they may set up using the Deep Strike special rule in any mission in which it is permitted.

Slow and Purposeful: Obliterators are huge and ponderous. They advance in a methodical manner laying down a constant hail of fire. To represent this they always count as stationary when firing, even if they moved in the same turn.

They are slow, however, and move as if they were in difficult terrain when they are in open terrain (rolling 2D6 and selecting the highest), they never receive +1 Attack for charging, strike at Initiative 1 in close combat and may never choose to perform a Sweeping Advance.

Daemonkin: Obliterators have the following Daemonic Gifts: Daemonic Aura, Daemonic Resilience and Daemon Armour (both of these are already shown on the profile above).

Obliterators have dwelt too long in the Eye of Terror and have contracted a contagion that sears their flesh to their armour. Marine and armour become one entity, growing down the centuries into hulking, weirdly baroque leviathans able to reshape their forms to spew death at their enemies. Obliterators are no longer even Chaos Space Marines instead they are an amalgam of Marine, Daemon and Armour, each part inseparable from the rest.

TROOPS

Chaos Space Marines, or Traitor Marines, were once loyal Space Marines, charged with defending Mankind in the name of the Emperor. They have since renounced their vows of loyalty and allied themselves with the dark gods of Chaos, putting their own selfish lust for power above all else. Their armour, weapons and even their physical form have changed to reflect their new loyalties and the darkness of their souls. Now, Mankind has no greater enemy than its own fallen protectors.

Chaos Space Marines

	Pts/Model	WS	BS	S	T	W	I	A	Ld	Sv
Chaos Space Marine	14	4	4	4	4	1	4	1	9	3+
Aspiring Champion	+13	4	4	4	4	1	4	2	10	3+

Number/squad: 5-20

Weapons: Each model may have a close combat weapon and either a bolter or a bolt pistol..

Options: One Chaos Space Marine may be armed with one of the following heavy weapons: lascannon at +15 pts; missile launcher at +10 pts; autocannon at +10 pts; heavy bolter at +5 pts.

One Chaos Space Marine may be armed with one of the following special weapons: plasma gun at +10 pts; meltagun at +10 pts; flamer at +6 pts; plasma pistol at +10 pts. If no heavy weapon is chosen, then an additional Chaos Space Marine may select a special weapon.

The entire squad may be armed with frag grenades at +1 pt per model and/or krak grenades at +2 pts per model.

A Chaos Space Marine unit may be given a Mark of Chaos (see special rules) and may have one or more Veteran skills. Note that if a unit is given a Mark of Chaos then its weapon options may change. See the Books of Chaos for more details.

Character: The squad may be led by an Aspiring Champion at +13 pts. The Aspiring Champion has access to the Chaos Armoury.

Transport: If the squad numbers ten Chaos Space Marines or less then it may be mounted in a Rhino for 50pts (see the Rhino transport entry on page 25 for more details).

Khorne Berzerkers

Berzerkers are Chaos Space Marines dedicated to the worship of Khorne. They are frightening, unrelenting warriors who fight with a manic frenzy to claim skulls for the Skull Throne of Khorne. Every member of the World Eaters Legion is a Berzerker, although not every Berzerker originates from that Legion. Many Chaos Warriors feel the call of Khorne appealing alternately to their martial pride and their vengeful bloodlust and become Berzerkers as a consequence.

Berzerkers are Chaos Space Marines with the Mark of Khorne. Lords and Lieutenants, Chosen, Possessed, Chaos Space Marines and Bikers can all bear the Mark of Khorne (see the Book of Khorne for full details). Chaos Space Marine squads which are given the Mark of Khorne will become an Elites choice unless the army is led by a model with the same mark in which case they remain a Troops choice.

Slaanesh Noise Marines

Noise Marines are followers of Slaanesh who crave all manner of visceral sensation. Their practices are both despicable and unspeakable, their history of atrocity going all the way back to the Horus Heresy. Their cravings have led to the use of a range of sonic weapons. Noise Marines hear the subtlest changes in pitch and volume and this in turn affects their brain, causing extreme emotional reactions. The louder and more discordant the noise, the greater the effect. Most Noise Marines originate from the Emperor's Children Legion although this is not exclusively the case. The seductive power of Slaanesh is such that new renegades are frequently drawn into his service.

Noise Marines are Chaos Space Marines with the Mark of Slaanesh. Lords and Lieutenants, Chosen, Possessed, Chaos Space Marines, Bikers and Chaos Havocs can all bear the Mark of Slaanesh. See the Book of Slaanesh for more details. Chaos Space Marine squads which are given the Mark of Slaanesh will become an Elites choice unless the army is led by a model with the same Mark in which case they remain a Troops choice.

Nurgle Plague Marines

Plague Marines are followers of Nurgle who have chosen to be the vessel for all manner of contagion and pestilence in return for immunity from their effects. Bloated and diseased Plague Marines are horrific to behold but can endure tremendous punishment thanks to Grandfather Nurgle's blessings. The Death Guard Legion was the sole source of all the original Plague Marines although since the Heresy there have been many whose will to live was strong enough to make them sacrifice their souls for continued existence.

Plague Marines are Chaos Space Marines with the Mark of Nurgle. Lords and Lieutenants, Chosen, Possessed, Chaos Space Marines and Chaos Havocs can all bear the Mark of Nurgle, see the Book of Nurgle for more details. Chaos Space Marine squads which are given the Mark of Nurgle will become an Elites choice unless the army is led by a model with the same Mark in which case they remain a Troops choice.

Thousand Sons

The Thousand Sons Legion of Chaos Space Marines serves Tzeentch and has always included many Sorcerers capable of wielding powerful psychic energies. Since the Heresy many other initiates with a talent for sorcery have turned to Tzeentch but there is one category of warrior that will always be unique to the Legion. In an attempt to arrest fast-spreading mutation within the Legion the Sorcerer Ahriman cast a spell known as the Rubric of Ahriman, which was so potent that every member of the Thousand Sons who was not a Sorcerer was turned to dust and bound forever in his armour as a disembodied spirit.

Thousand Sons fall into two categories, although all bear the Mark of Tzeentch. Lords, Lieutenants, Chosen and Possessed are Sorcerers. Normal Chaos Space Marine squads are instead disembodied spirits trapped within their power armour (although unit Aspiring Champions are still Sorcerers). See the Book of Tzeentch for more details.

Chaos Space Marine squads which are given the Mark of Tzeentch will become an Elites choice unless the army is led by a model with the same Mark in which case they remain a Troops choice.

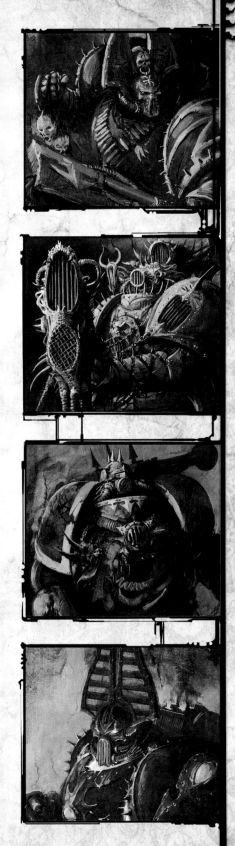

There is no limit to the number of rapacious warp entities eager to feast on the flesh and souls of the living. They have infinite different forms and equally infinite malice. Each of the Chaos Gods has their own favourite servants however and it is these who fill the ranks of their Daemon armies, waging eternal war for the glory of the infernal masters and their own vindictive satisfaction.

Daemon Packs

	Pts/Model	WS	BS	S	T	W	I	A	Ld	Sv
Bloodletter	26	4	0	5	4	1	4	2	10	3/5+
Plaguebearer	16	4	0	4	4(5)	1	4	2	8	-/5+
Horror	17	2	3	4	3	2	2	1	8	-/5+
Daemonette	15	4	0	4	3	1	4	1+1	8	-/5+

Number/squad: 5-15

Weapons: Each type of Daemon has a range of daemonic abilities. Some of these are innate, others are conferred by the weapons they carry.

SPECIAL RULES

Bloodletters of Khorne fight with great warp-forged Hellblades, which function like power weapons. They are clad in the Brass Armour of Khorne and receive a 3+ armour save. They must charge and make a sweeping advance whenever possible.

Horrors of Tzeentch use the Daemonic Fire ability to hurl sorcerous flames at their enemies. Any number of Horrors may be upgraded to Flamers of Tzeentch at +6 points per model. Flamers have the same profile but instead of the Daemonic Fire gift, have the ability to use Doombolt with no Psychic test required.

Daemonettes of Slaanesh can use the Warp Scream ability (see the Book of Slaanesh on page 59) and have Daemonic Talons.

Plaguebearers of Nurgle carry Nurgle's Rot (see Book of Nurgle) and have the Daemonic Venom ability representing the virulent slime that seeps from their knives and talons, (note that the extra attack is already included in their profile above).

Summoned: Daemon packs are always summoned to the battlefield. See the Summoning special rule for more details.

Invulnerable: Daemons are unnatural creatures, made from the very stuff of Chaos itself and are therefore very difficult to destroy. They all have the Daemonic Aura ability and have a 5+ Invulnerable save in addition to the normal armour save shown on their profile.

Instability: Daemon packs are subject to Daemonic Instability, see p.12 for more details.

Nurglings

	Pts/Model	WS	BS	S	T	W	I	A	Ld	Sv
Nurglings	10	3	0	3	3	3	3	3	7	5+

Number/squad: 3-10 Nurgling bases.

Weapons: Claws and teeth

SPECIAL RULES

Invulnerable. Nurglings are unnatural creatures, made from the very stuff of Chaos itself and are therefore very difficult to destroy. The saving throw on their profile is therefore Invulnerable.

Vulnerable to blasts: Template, Ordnance and Blast marker weapons inflict two wounds instead of one on Nurglings. A weapon of Strength 6 or higher will of course kill a Nurgling base outright, assuming they fail their Invulnerable save in accordance with the Instant Death rule.

Small Target: Being extremely hard to hit in cover Nurglings' cover save is at +1. Note this doesn't give them a cover save if they wouldn't normally get one. Because of their diminutive size they do not block line of sight to anything behind or with them other than more Nurglings.

Children of Father Nurgle: Nurglings tend to follow in the shadow of the Champions of Nurgle consequently an army may only include one unit of Nurglings for each Independent Character or Unit with the Mark of Nurgle.

Mischievous: A unit of Nurglings cannot be trusted to hold an objective as they will inevitably wander off or try to damage it. Consequently they may never hold table quarters or objectives.

Instability. Nurglings are subject to Daemonic Instability, see special rules for more details.

Nurglings are the creations of the Chaos god Nurgle. They caper across the battlefield in a putrescent tide, highlighted by a babbling cacophony of shrieks, seeking to drag larger opponents down with their infection-riddled claws and venomous bites.

FAST ATTACK

At the time of the Horus Heresy, the Adeptus Astartes made very limited use of jump packs. Those that escaped to the Eye of Terror with theirs were a rare breed who, after millennia swooping and soaring in the burning skies of Daemon Worlds, became a faction that cut across the boundaries of the Traitor Legions, unified by the thrill of the hunt. Down the centuries their equipment has mutated in the way of Chaos, fusing the original machinery with daemonic power. Now their battle cries are amplified to project a howling scream that drives their prey before them.

0-1 Chaos Raptors

	Pts/Model	WS	BS	S	T	W	I	A	Ld	Sv
Raptor	29	4	4	4	4	1	4	1	9	3+
Aspiring Champion	+13	4	4	4	4	1	4	2	10	3+

Number/squad: 5-10

Weapons: Bolt pistol and close combat weapon, frag and krak grenades.

Options: Up to three models in the unit may be armed with one of the following weapons: plasma gun at +10 pts; meltagun at +10 pts; flamer at +6 pts; plasma pistol at +10 pts.

A Raptor unit may be given the Mark of Chaos Undivided and may have one or more Veteran skills.

Character: One squad member may be upgraded to an Aspiring Champion for +13 pts. The Aspiring Champion may select additional equipment from the Chaos Armoury.

SPECIAL RULES

Daemonkin: Raptors have the Daemonic Flight and Daemonic Visage gifts and may use the Hit and Run rule.

Hit and Run: At the end of a round of close combat the Raptors may choose to break off if they and at least some of their close combat opponents do not have to fall back. The unit falls back 3D6" in any direction and automatically regroups at the end of the move (regardless of enemy within 6" or being below half strength). Enemy models that were in close combat with them before the break-off may only consolidate.

Chaos Space Marine Bikers

	Pts/Model	WS	BS	S	T	W	I	A	Ld	Sv
Chaos Biker	34	4	4	4	4(5)	1	4	2	9	3+
Aspiring Champion	+13	4	4	4	4(5)	1	4	3	10	3+

Number/squad: 3-10

Weapons: Each bike is fitted with twin-linked bolters. Each Chaos Space Marine rider is armed with a bolt pistol or a close combat weapon. Note that they may not use an additional close combat weapon due to the need to control the bike.

Options: The squad may have frag grenades at +1 pt and krak grenades at +2 pts per model.

Up to two Chaos Space Marine Bikers may replace their twin linked bolters with a meltagun or plasma gun at +10 pts or a flamer at + 6 pts.

A Biker unit may be given a Mark of Chaos (see special rules) and may have one or more Veteran skills.

Character: The squad may be led by an Aspiring Champion at +13 pts. The Aspiring Champion may select additional equipment from the Chaos Armoury.

SPECIAL RULES
Iron Steeds. Like all bike-mounted models, Chaos Bikers get +1 Toughness. Additionally their bikes are covered in spikes, granting them +1 Attack. These modifications are already included in the profile above.

Chaos Space Marine Bikers get no additional benefit from the Daemonic Resilience ability, which is not cumulative with the Bike bonus.

There was a time when bikes were simply another piece of equipment to the Traitor Legions but years within the Warp have changed this. The bike is almost an extension of its rider, both covered in cruel spikes and jutting horns. The roar of the bike's engine is the growl of a snarling beast that fires the damned soul of its rider to acts of greater recklessness. They trail brimstone and death in their wake as the harbingers of the dark legions.

Daemonic Beasts

	Pts/Model	WS	BS	S	T	W	I	A	Ld	Sv
Flesh Hounds	21	4	0	5	4	1	5	2	8	-/5+
Screamers	15	4	0	4	4	1	5	1	8	-/5+
Furies	15	4	0	5	4	1	5	2	7	-/5+

Pack: 5-10 beasts. A Daemonic Beasts pack may only contain one type of Daemon.

Weapons: Claws and Fangs.

SPECIAL RULES
Flesh Hounds of Khorne. Flesh Hounds wear Collars of Khorne (see Book of Khorne) and move as Cavalry. Flesh Hounds must always charge and make a sweeping advance whenever possible.

Screamers of Tzeentch. Because they rely on a single swift pass to claim their prey they have the Furious Charge Veteran skill. Additionally, they have the Daemonic Flight ability.

At the end of a round of close combat a unit of Screamers must break off if it and at least some of its close combat opponents do not have to fall back. The unit falls back 3D6" in any direction and automatically regroups at the end of the move (regardless of enemy within 6" or being below half strength). Enemy models that were in close combat with them before the break-off may only consolidate.

Furies. Alone among the commoner varieties of Daemonkind Furies are aligned with Chaos Undivided. They have the Daemonic Flight ability.

Summoned. Daemonic Beasts are summoned onto the battlefield as described in the rules at the start of the Chaos army list.

Invulnerable. Daemons are unnatural creatures formed from the very stuff of Chaos itself and are very difficult to destroy. They all have Daemonic Auras and are treated as being Invulnerable and may make a 5+ save against any and all wounds they take.

Instability. Daemonic Beasts are subject to Daemonic Instability; see special rules for more details.

Many of the more primal Daemonic entities are used as hunting beasts by the Traitor Legions. Whilst they lack the calculating evil of their anthromorphic kin, they combine feral cunning and bestial power in the most terrifying way.

Chaos Havocs

	Pts/Model	WS	BS	S	T	W	I	A	Ld	Sv
Chaos Space Marine	14	4	4	4	4	1	4	1	9	3+
Aspiring Champion	+13	4	4	4	4	1	4	2	10	3+

Number/squad: 5-10

Weapons: Close combat weapon and either a bolter or a bolt pistol..

Options: Up to four members of the squad may replace their boltgun with a weapon from the following list: lascannon at +35 pts; missile launcher at + 20 pts; autocannon at +20 pts; heavy bolter at +15 pts; plasma gun at +15 pts; meltagun at +15 pts; flamer at +10 pts

A Havoc unit may be given a Mark of Chaos (see special rules) and may have one or more Veteran skills. Note that if a unit is given a Mark of Chaos then its weapon options may change. See the Books of Chaos for more details.

Character: One member of the squad may become an Aspiring Champion at +13 pts. The Aspiring Champion may select additional equipment from the Chaos Armoury.

Transport: If the squad totals ten Chaos Space Marines or less it may be mounted in a Rhino armoured carrier at the additional cost of 50 pts.

Chaos Havocs are Chaos Space Marines with a preference for killing at range with their powerful weaponry. Each Chaos Havoc's heavy weapon is a trusted ally of a thousand battles, its wielder completely familiar with its every operation. Together, weapon and Chaos Space Marine touch every part of the battlefield with death and destruction, laying waste to their enemies like capricious gods.

Chaos Predator

	Pts	Front Armour	Side Armour	Rear Armour	BS
Chaos Predator	85	13	11	10	4

Type: Tank   **Crew:** Chaos Space Marines

Weapons: The Chaos Predator is armed with one turret-mounted weapon from the following list: twin-linked lascannon at +35 pts or an autocannon at +15 pts.

Options: The Chaos Predator may be upgraded with a pair of side sponsons, each armed with one of the following weapons: heavy bolter at +10 pts for the pair, or a lascannon at +25 pts for the pair.

The Predator may be equipped with any vehicle upgrades allowed from the Chaos Space Marine Armoury.

The Predators of the Chaos Legions are a legacy of pre-Heresy times, although now they are barely recognisable to those familiar with the Imperial version. Daemonic maws adorn every gun barrel, dark icons cover every surface and their hulls are twisted and mutated.

I was born the sixth son of Kaschada, hetman of the Tabor on the day that the Great Prophet came among us. The Tabor were the outcasts of the world, condemned because we were faithful to the Gods of the Four Winds: the Blood Wind that fired the warrior's soul, the Plague Wind that purged the weak, the Wind of Change that brought the gifts of the Gods to men and the Scented Wind that roused the passions.

Our enemies were the Otman, men of the cities who served the Sky God. For centuries they had scoured the grasslands, hunting us down, but with the coming of the Prophet that all changed.

In my fourteenth year, I was part of the horde that swept into the city of Jaghann and put the inhabitants to the slaughter. Those were great days; the Tabor were masters of the wide grasslands, raiding and plundering at our pleasure. I owned four gold-chased pistols and a fine Qaseen sabre. I flew my hawks, wore robes of silk and accepted no

insult from any man. One by one the cities of the Otman fell before us and great caravans of slaves stretched across the plains to the mountain of the Prophet, for sacrifice to the winds.

The prophet was a man like no other; taller than any of the Tabor, he wore armour of jet and gold, his great gauntlet could shatter any barred gate and his blade could cut even Qaseen steel. No man could meet his burning gaze and the hetmen of the clans learned from him of the true nature of the Gods and how to bring death to our enemies.

Finally, our host met with the Otman army on the Red Grass. Standing with the enemy were twenty Storm Giants, heroes of the Otman who it was said had travelled beyond the winds to the citadel of the Sky God and had now returned to save their people from our wrath. The Prophet told us that immortality would be the reward for those who bested them.

Chaos Dreadnought

	Pts	WS	BS	S	Armour Front	Side	Rear	I	A
Dreadnought	75	4	4	6(10)	12	12	10	4	3

Type: Walker   **Crew:** One Chaos Space Marine

Weapons: The Chaos Dreadnought is armed with a Dreadnought close combat weapon incorporating a twin-linked bolter in one arm and one weapon from the following list in the other: twin-linked autocannon at +35 pts; twin-linked lascannon at + 50 pts; twin-linked heavy bolter at +30 pts; multi-melta at +40 pts, or a plasma cannon at +40 pts.

Options: Instead of a ranged weapon, a Chaos Dreadnought can have an additional Dreadnought close combat weapon incorporating a twin-linked bolter at +15 pts. This will add +1 to the number of Attacks on the profile above. It is unlikely this component will be made for the Dreadnought but is included for those interested in doing conversions. If used, neither arm can be replaced with a missile launcher.

A single twin-linked bolter may be upgraded to a heavy flamer at an extra cost of +12 pts. The Dreadnought may replace one close combat arm (along with its twin-linked bolter) with a missile launcher at an additional cost of +10 pts. This reduces its Attacks characteristic to 2, its Strength to 6, and it no longer counts as being armed with a Dreadnought close combat weapon.

The Dreadnought may be equipped with any vehicle upgrades and Gifts allowed from the Chaos Space Marine Armoury.

SPECIAL RULES

Fire Frenzy. At the start of the Movement phase, before moving the Dreadnought roll on the chart below for each Dreadnought which is either mobile or has at least one functioning weapon system:

1   **Blood Rage.** The Dreadnought may not fire this turn, but instead must move 6+D6" towards the nearest enemy model or unit. The Dreadnought must assault this unit in the Assault phase if able, and will double its basic Attacks characteristic. If already in close combat, the Dreadnought will continue to fight with double its Attacks characteristic. If the Dreadnought is immobilised and not in close combat treat this result as Fire Frenzy.

2-5   Move and shoot normally.

6   **Fire Frenzy.** The Dreadnought may not move or assault this turn, but instead must shoot all of its weapons TWICE at the nearest enemy model or unit. If no enemy targets are visible or in range it will fire at the nearest friendly unit that is visible and in range instead. If the Dreadnought has no functioning weapons or no possible targets in range treat this result as Blood Rage instead.

My soul called for the blood of these warriors and I charged gladly into battle. Over that long day I charged five times, each time I fired every pistol but to no effect – the Storm Giants' armour was proof against my bullets. In each charge I saw their guns cut through our squadrons, piling great heaps of men and horses before their lines. The evening sky turned blood red and the air stank of death. The great horde of the Tabor, the sons of the Prophet, was all but destroyed, my father was dead, my brothers were dead. I was wounded and my fine sabre broken yet my hatred for my enemies was greater than ever. We prepared for one more charge, no longer in squadrons but a scattering of bloodied individuals, awaiting a sign from the Prophet.

Instead of raising the banner to signal another charge he pointed to the crest of the hill at his back as the moon rose behind it. Over the ridge came daemons with blood-soaked skin bearing huge axes and swords. They rushed at the Storm Giants and we followed. The Warriors of the Gods clashed and normal men

were hurled about by the power they unleashed. I staggered into the press clutching a broken lance. Flaming winds cast me down but I pressed on and thrust my lance into the first of the Storm Giants I could reach. I struck him where his armour was twisted and melted. He fell and as he did the Prophet leapt upon him and with glowing blade cut him open and pulled the organs from his body. He held his bloody prizes aloft and told me that immortality beckoned me.

Scarcely a hundred Tabor had survived the battle. The Prophet asked me what I felt. I told him that I wanted vengeance, vengeance against the giants who had killed my father and brothers, against those who had shattered my clan, vengeance against their kin and their young, that I wanted to tear down their God and make them regret raising arms against the Tabor. The Prophet was pleased with my answer and said that I would travel beyond the winds with him and that I would also be a warrior of the Gods.

Whilst in the Imperium the Dreadnought is a living icon venerating a great warrior from the past, in the Chaos Legions the Dreadnought is a symbol of the unending pain and torment of the damned. The occupants of these infernal sarcophagi are kept alive but are in constant howling agony. Inevitable insanity does not curb the pain and within each machine the Chaos Space Marine rages against the world outside, a terrifying and unpredictable beast that needs to be shackled when not in battle.

Chaos Land Raider

	Pts	Front Armour	Side Armour	Rear Armour	BS
Chaos Land Raider	250	14	14	14	4

Type: Tank

Crew: Chaos Space Marines

Weapons: The Chaos Land Raider is armed with two twin-linked lascannon and a twin-linked heavy bolter.

Options: The Chaos Land Raider may be equipped with any of the vehicle upgrades and Gifts allowed from the Chaos Space Marine Armoury.

Transport: The Chaos Land Raider can carry up to ten Chaos Space Marines, or five Chaos Space Marine Terminators.

Fire Points - 0: The Land Raider is a vehicle of ancient design, and represents the pinnacle of armoured vehicle technology. As such, the protection afforded by its inches thick, massively armoured hull cannot be compromised by extraneous hatches and firing ports. The top hatches are for the use of the Land Raider's crew, and cannot be used by passengers as firing ports.

Access Points – 3: The Land Raider has a large frontal access ramp and a hatch on each side of the hull, any of which may be used to embark or disembark.

Notes: There are two special features of the Land Raider that are made possible by the Possessing Spirit. This is a daemonic presence that replaces the Machine Spirit in Land Raiders dedicated to Chaos.

Fire Control: The Chaos Space Marine gunner is assisted in selecting and targeting the enemy by the possessing force of the Infernal Device. The vehicle may always fire one additional weapon system to those it would normally be able to fire (assuming it isn't already firing them all and that it is entitled to fire at the speed it is moving). This shot may be targeted against a different target to that engaged by the crew. Automatic targeting is less accurate than if directed by a crewman and is conducted with BS2. If the crew are stunned or shaken and unable to fire, the possessing force of the Infernal Device may still fire a weapon using this rule.

Infernal Device: If the crew are stunned and unable to direct the Land Raider, then the possessing force of the Infernal Device will take over temporarily. The Land Raider may be moved directly ahead in a straight line up to its maximum move,

Land Raiders are immobilised by difficult terrain as normal.

Blood jetted from the headless guardsman's neck, his severed skull gripped in the fist of the red-armoured giant before him. Lasbolts exploded around the blood-splattered warrior, scoring deep grooves in his battered armour, but Korgha the Slaughterman paid them no mind, hacking all about him with his howling glaive. Death surrounded him, blood flowed and the sky burned red with horror. Howling madness engulfed him as he chopped limbs from bodies, skewered men on his glaive and beheaded foes by the dozen. The World Eaters followed their champion into battle, cutting down terrified guardsmen as they went, uncaring of the shots that felled dozens of their number. Those that fell struck out even as they died, hacking their own axes across their necks that the lord Khorne might have yet more skulls for his brass throne.

Swords, rifles and fists thundered against Korgha's body, dragging howls of rage and bloodlust from his lips as he slaughtered his foe. Shadows flitted before him, indistinct in the red haze that filled his vision. Heedless of whether he killed friend or foe, Korgha swung the glaive in giant, disembowelling strokes. Nothing could stop him – he was a living engine of death, killing and killing, feeding the hunger for bloodshed that empowered him. His glaive smoked, as though fresh from the furnace, boiling the blood of its victims, the daemon bound within its blade ripping their souls screaming from their bodies. Bound for millennia within the weapon, it railed against its imprisonment, goading its bearer to frenzied slaughter, and feeding vicariously on Korgha's unquenchable bloodlust. It gorged itself on the bloodshed, the blood of the living all that could sate its monstrous hunger for slaughter in the name of Khorne.

The daemon sensed a shift in Korgha's aggression, feeling the bloodlust seep from his shattered flesh. Its champion's armour was burned and rent asunder, his lifeblood spilling from a score of fatal wounds. There were enemies yet to slay, but his shattered body had not the strength to fight and the daemon howled in fury. Korgha's body spasmed with the daemon's anger, screaming his frustration to the sky. The daemon seized its chance, bringing up Korgha's arm and showing the champion its crimson edge. Korgha smiled even as death claimed him, chopping the gore-smeared blade across his neck. The daemon tasted the champion's death, knowing that Khorne cared not from whence the blood flowed.

All that mattered was that it flowed...

Chaos Defiler

	Pts	WS	BS	S	Front	Side	Rear	I	A
					Armour				
Defiler	150	2	4	8	12	12	10	4	2

Type: Walker **Crew:** Bound Daemon

Weapons: The Defiler is armed with a battle cannon, a reaper autocannon and a heavy flamer (actually two flamers firing as one). Because of its Daemonic nature it counts as a monstrous creature in close combat.

Options: The Daemon Engine automatically has the Daemonic Possession vehicle upgrade so ignores any shaken or stunned damage results it suffers.

The heavy flamer can be upgraded to a havoc launcher at +10 points or replaced with the Living Vehicle upgrade at +10 points. The only way either of these vehicle upgrades can be used on the Defiler is as replacements for the heavy flamer. Any other vehicle upgrades are bought as normal from the Chaos Space Marine armoury.

The reaper autocannon can be replaced by twin-linked heavy bolters at no extra cost or by twin-linked lascannons at +30 points.

SPECIAL RULES
Indirect Fire. A Defiler can be configured to be able to fire indirectly as well as directly. This costs +25 points. When fired in this way the Battle Cannon becomes a Barrage (ie, Guess range) weapon with a range of 36" to 72". Strength and AP are unaffected.

The Defiler was fashioned at the command of Abaddon the Despoiler. It is a six-legged baroquely-forged machine with savage hooks and barbs along its limbs. Shrouded in noxious fumes, its engine a bestial growl, the Defiler lays waste to the ground it drives over and batters down the strongest defences with its mighty battle cannon.

THE BOOKS OF CHAOS

There are many paths to damnation and the four great Chaos Powers, Khorne, Nurgle, Slaanesh and Tzeentch all have their own worshippers among the Chaos Space Marine Legions. In addition there are Chaos Space Marines who worship all four as a Pantheon known as Chaos Undivided.

The Books of Chaos detail the Marks and Gifts of each of the Chaos powers. Each Book follows a similar format.

- The ethos of the Chaos God and his worshippers.
- The Mark of the Chaos God and its effects.
- The gifts that can be bestowed on models bearing the Mark of the Chaos God, in addition to those in the basic Chaos Armoury. Remember that Gifts of the Gods count towards a character's wargear limit.
- Psychic powers peculiar to the Chaos God.
- Weaponry variations for the followers of the Chaos God.

Applying Chaos Marks

Each of the Chaos Powers favours a particular style of fighting and this influences which unit types can bear their Mark. The table below summarises which Marks can be granted to which models.

Vehicles can be dedicated to one of the four Chaos powers but this is not really the same thing as bearing a Mark. Instead the vehicle has an upgrade peculiar to the God it is dedicated to. Transport vehicles which do not occupy force organisation chart selections (such as the Rhino) may only be dedicated to a God if the unit they were purchased for bears the Mark of the same god.

Ancient Enemies

For millennia, the Chaos gods have vied and competed amongst each other for power over the mortal realms, and great rivalries and hatreds have formed between followers of gods with opposite aims. For this reason, an army led by a character with the Mark of Khorne cannot contain any units or characters with the Mark of Slaanesh, Daemons of Slaanesh, or vehicles dedicated to Slaanesh; likewise an army led by a Slaaneshi character cannot have any Khornate units. Similarly, an army led by a character with the Mark of Tzeentch cannot contain units, daemons of vehicles marked by Nurgle, nor can a Nurgle-led army contain any Tzeentch units. An army led by a character with the Mark of Chaos Undivided, or no mark at all, has less cause to fear the wrath of an angry patron, so may field any units of any alignment in the army. An independent character with any mark except the Mark of Chaos Undivided may not join a unit with a different mark.

Favoured Units

Each Chaos God has a sacred number. These are 9 for Tzeentch, 8 for Khorne, 7 for Nurgle and 6 for Slaanesh

Retinues, squads and packs that bear the Mark of one of these deities and contain at the start of the battle the same number of models as that deitiy's sacred number (or an exact multiple of it) are said to be Favoured by the Gods. Note that Independent Characters leading retinues are counted for this purpose but Followers are not.

The Force Organisation Chart

If a unit which normally occupies a Troop, Fast Attack or Heavy Support choice on the force organisation chart is given a Mark of Chaos other than Chaos Undivided then it will become an Elite choice instead. If the Mark they bear is the same as the army'scommander they will continue to occupy the same force organisation choice they did before. The commander will be the Chaos Lord if there is one, otherwise the Chaos Lieutenant who costs the most points. If neither of these are present then an Aspiring Champion acting as host for a Greater Daemon commands, or rather passes on the Greater Daemon's wishes.

	Undivided	Khorne	Nurgle	Slaanesh	Tzeentch
Lords or Lieutenants	Yes	Yes	Yes	Yes	Yes
Chosen	Yes	Yes	Yes	Yes	Yes
Possessed Chaos Space Marines	Yes	Yes	Yes	Yes	Yes
Chaos Space Marines	Yes	Yes	Yes	Yes	Yes
Chaos Bikes	Yes	Yes	No	Yes	No
Chaos Raptors	Yes	No	No	No	No
Chaos Havocs	Yes	No	Yes	Yes	No

The Mark of Chaos Undivided

The four major powers of Chaos form a pantheon of gods, with many followers seduced by the attentions of one specific deity. Many others however, worship Chaos in its undiluted glory, paying tribute to, and drawing their powers through, the primal essence of the Warp itself. As each Chaos power reflects a specific facet of human nature, some propose Chaos Undivided represents the infinite depths of evil that gnaw at the very roots of the mortal soul.

Men are not given to understand such matters, and the diverse followings of Chaos Undivided worship it in many different forms.

In its most literal sense, Chaos Undivided is a pantheon of gods; the four major powers occupying opposing points on a compass. When a follower worships he may direct his tributes to the god most able to answer his pleas. Such a follower may receive the blessings of each of the gods at different times, but is unlikely to gain the favour granted to an individual dedicated wholly to one power. The cultist may also honour the minor spirits of the Warp if he feels they may be able to aid him. These beings are insignificant compared to the four major gods, but often have their own petty agendas in which they will attempt to ensnare the unwary.

Others worship Chaos Undivided as a single entity. They perceive the various powers as merely aspects of one vast, malevolent intelligence which mortals cannot hope to engage on any but the most basic level. These followers may ally themselves with the other powers, but will never give themselves fully to one god, seeking instead to follow a purer form of devotion to Chaos in its unadulterated whole.

Another form of worship of Chaos Undivided may be seen in those who look to use Chaos to their own ends, and seek only temporary pacts with the powers. These misguided individuals see their own ambitions as above those of the chaos powers. This is the ultimate gamble, with but two possible outcomes: daemonhood or damnation.

The Mark of Chaos Undivided costs +5 points for an independent character or +1 point per model in a unit and allows the character/unit to re-roll all failed Morale checks. Only one re-roll can be made and the new result is final. To benefit from the re-roll, all members of the unit that is testing must have the Mark of Chaos Undivided or be Followers or Steeds of a model that has.

Fabius Bile

Fabius Bile was once Lieutenant Commander of the Emperor's Children and he accompanied them during the Siege of Terra when, rather than battling for the Palace, they committed terrible atrocities on the civilian population. Bile took advantage of the situation to conduct horrific experiments and was responsible for altering the brain chemistry of the Emperor's Children to make them more responsive to extreme stimulus. He did not follow them in their worship of Slaanesh though. Instead he distanced himself from his Legion and devoted himself to researching forbidden technology unlocking the secrets behind the creation of the Space Marines.

Over the following centuries Bile travelled the galaxy offering his services as the self-styled 'Primogenitor' to Traitor commanders in return for prisoners or ancient technical libra. His ability to transform normal soldiers into ravening beasts with his serums and create armies using the black technology of cloning was so invaluable that any price would be paid. As a consequence genocide and genetic debasement marked his path and the Inquisition still strives to eliminate the threat of his genetically enhanced, psychotic, 'new men' from systems throughout the Imperium.

After narrowly escaping the Emperor's justice at the hands of the Salamanders Chapter in the Arden system he secured a base of operations on one of the crone worlds within the Eye of Terror. Here he has forged alliances with each of the Traitor Legions, providing them with the expertise they need to create new Chaos Space Marines in return for their protection.

	Points	D6 roll	WS	BS	S	T	W	I	A	Ld	Sv
	114	1	6	3	5	4	3	5	4	10	3+
Fabius Bile	114	2-5	5	4	4	4	3	4	3	10	3+
	114	6	3	5	3	5	4	3	3	10	3+

A Chaos Space Marine army may include Fabius Bile. If you decide to take him then he counts as the Chaos Lord choice for the army. He must be used exactly as described below and may not be given extra equipment from the Chaos Armoury.

Wargear: Rod of Torment, Xyclos Needler, bolt pistol, frag & krak grenades, Chirurgeon and the Mark of Chaos Undivided.

SPECIAL RULES
Characteristics: Fabius Bile has probably subjected himself to more experimentation than any other creature. To represent the fact that his physical capabilities vary tremendously according to his most recent undertaking, Fabius Bile's characteristic profile is generated randomly before each game (preferably in the presence of your opponent). Roll a D6 to determine which profile is used. This profile will not remain constant and is re-rolled before each game.

The Chirurgeon: This is a complex, part magical, part technological device which is attached to Bile's spine and extends its spidery limbs over his shoulders. It pumps life-giving black ichor around his body, charged with the immortal energy of the Warp. The direct effects of this in the game are to give Fabius a 4+ invulnerable save against any wounds he suffers.

Xyclos Needler: This gun fires a dart of virulent poison into the victim's blood stream. It has the following profile:

Rng: 12"   Str: n/a   AP: 6   Assault 3

The weapon does not have a Strength value as such, and always wounds on a D6 roll of 2+. The Needler counts as having a Strength of 1 if fired at a vehicle.

Rod of Torment: The daemon-forged Rod of Torment amplifies the slightest pin prick into a raging weal of agony. The Rod of Torment counts as a close combat weapon. However, any opponent suffering one or more wounds from the Rod of Torment is immediately disabled by the pain and removed as a casualty even if they have any remaining wounds.

Independent Character: Fabius is an independent character and follows all the independent character special rules as given in the Warhammer 40,000 rulebook.

Enhanced Warriors: If Fabius Bile is the commander of a force he can enhance some of the warriors under his control through genetic manipulation and drugs. For +3 points per model, any number of Chaos Space Marine squads without a Mark of Chaos (and **only** Chaos Space Marine squads - not Bikers, Raptors, or any other unit) can be 'enhanced' by Bile's treatment.

SPECIAL RULES
Genetic Corruption: Fabius' attempts to enhance his warriors don't always work out as well as he hoped. To represent this, at the start of the battle, after both sides have set up but before the first turn takes place, roll a D6 for each enhanced squad and consult the table below.

D6	Result
1	**Berserk Rage!** The warriors attack each other in an animalistic fury. Make an Armour save for each warrior, removing any who fail. Those who are removed will count as casualties for the purposes of calculating Victory points. Survivors are at +1 Strength.
2-5	**Stable Mutation.** Bile's experiments have proved successful (this time) and the Enhanced Warriors are at +1 Strength and Initiative.
6	**Created a Monster.** The abilities of each warrior are temporarily enhanced to superhuman levels. Each warrior adds +1 to his Strength, Initiative and Attacks characteristics. Unfortunately, not even the Enhanced Warriors' constitutions can withstand this level of performance for long, and after the battle the Warriors will die. Any who survive the battle will count as casualties for the purposes of calculating Victory points.

Alpha Legion

The Alpha Legion was the last of the First Founding Chapters and from its inception was determined to prove its worth relative to the older Legions. Their Primarch, Alpharius perpetuated this rivalry and encouraged self-reliance, discipline and innovative tactics in his Legion. The Alpha Legion respected strength and despised the weak. They were drawn to the strength of Warmaster Horus and welcomed the opportunity to test themselves against their brother Space Marines. Although they joined the Heresy the Alpha Legion stayed distinct from the other Traitor Legions and fought its own campaign. Since the Heresy they have remained independent, setting up their own network of cults and pursuing separate objectives.

Tactically, the Alpha Legion believes in attacking from several directions at once. This requires careful planning and skilful infiltration. Extensive use is made of spies and corruption to weaken the enemy's resolve before any decisive move is made. Amongst the Traitor Legions the Alpha Legion makes most use of cultist troops. As they tend to operate as raiders deep within the Imperium they need local support to bolster their numbers. Considerable effort is expended to spread propaganda to incite revolt and acts of sabotage. When the Alpha Legion is committed to action events tend to move very quickly. The Legion attaches great importance to its field commanders, using their own initiative to outwit the enemy as this magnifies the advantages that Space Marines have over more conventional troops.

The Legion has great pride in its prowess and welcomes opportunities to demonstrate their superior skills against loyalist Space Marine Chapters. They have been known to hold back some of their forces to test themselves more thoroughly in these circumstances.

Many Alpha Legion operations are planned to encourage and support cultist activity. The Alpha Legion may therefore make use of the Cultist army list entry below as a Troops selection on the force organisation chart.

Chaos Cultists

The Cults that are sponsored and supported by the Alpha Legion are trained to assault and secure key objectives to ensure subsequent attacks by the Legion achieve complete surprise. They are skilled combatants who combine stealth with close combat. Heavy weapons will normally only slow them down so they are only equipped with assault weaponry.

	Pts/Model	WS	BS	S	T	W	I	A	Ld	Sv
Chaos Cultist	6	3	3	3	3	1	3	1	7	6+
Cult Champion	+5	3	3	3	3	1	3	2	8	6+

Number/squad: A Chaos Cult consists of between 10 and 20 Chaos Cultists.

Weapons: Each model has a close combat weapon and either a laspistol or autopistol.

Options: The entire squad may be armed with frag grenades at +1 point per model and/or krak grenades at +1 point per model and/or meltabombs at +2 points per model.

A Chaos Cult may bear the Mark of Chaos Undivided at +1 point per model. If it bears the Mark then one member can carry a Chaos Icon at no additional cost.

Character: The squad may be led by a Cult Champion at +5 points. The Cult Champion has access to the Chaos Armoury. He may have up to 10 points of items from the Weapons list.

SPECIAL RULES

A unit of Chaos Cultists serving the Alpha Legion must have one of the following skill sets:

- Scouts – Infiltrate and Move through Cover.
- Assassins – Infiltrate and Furious Charge.
- Saboteurs – Infiltrate and Siege Specialists.

There is no further points cost for these skills. See Veteran Skills special rules for more details on how the skills work.

Daemons: The Alpha Legion cannot normally rely on Daemons remaining stable for long enough for them to be useful because they are so far from the Eye of Terror. When operating on a world where they have secured the belief of Chaos cults they will gladly add Daemons to the diversity of their attacks. Because of this the Alpha Legion may include Daemon Packs but only Cultist units may carry Icons to summon them. Icons may not be carried by other units or bought as wargear by characters They may use Daemon Princes and Possessed Chaos Space Marines normally.

Infiltrators: Alpha Legionaries can only bear the Mark of Chaos Undivided and their Veterans are renowned for their Infiltration skills. Any Alpha Legion Chaos Space Marine in power armour (or Daemon armour) on foot may have the Infiltration skill at a cost of +5 points for independent characters or +1 point per other model. The Infiltration skill does not count toward their maximum number of skills.

Iron Warriors

The Iron Warriors are cold-hearted killers motivated by paranoia and selfishness. They trust their wargear but nothing else and since the Heresy have rarely allied with any other Legion. They are the consummate masters of siege warfare and fortification. Where they strike they fortify, establishing dominion over worlds from their impenetrable defences, daring the Imperium to drive them out. They are still led by their Primarch, Peturabo, now a mighty Daemon Prince from Medrenngard, their fortress-world deep in the Eye of Terror.

The Iron Warriors are the most heavily armed of the Chaos Legions. Because they are siege specialists they rely less on close combat and more on withering salvos of fire. Even when fighting outside fortifications their approach remains the same with the greatest importance being placed on a detailed fire plan. They are adept at quickly erecting formidable field fortifications. This is not done flippantly but is instead a careful tactic aimed at establishing strongpoints which will tie down superior numbers of enemy, allowing the Iron Warrior reserves to achieve superiority elsewhere. They are quite willing to allow strongpoints to be cut off, falling back before enemy assaults, confident that even when isolated the positions will be held. Enemy assaults can then be directed around the front-line defences into specially prepared killing fields in the second line. Only when they have destroyed the enemy momentum will they counter-attack but when launched the counter-attacks are extremely fierce. Offensively they are methodical, always seeking to grind down their opponents by attrition until the moment comes when they can be swept away by a concerted attack.

If attacking fortifications the Iron Warriors will quickly decide at what point they will actually attack, then they will launch a series of feint attacks designed to confuse the enemy and encourage them to weaken the real objective.

- The only Mark they can bear is the Mark of Chaos Undivided.

- Iron Warrior armies may not include any Daemons apart from Daemon Princes and Possessed Chaos Space Marines (although their Possessed are unusual in that they harness bound Daemonic energies to power an array of cybernetic enhancements).

- Inevitably Iron Warriors are all excellent siege fighters so every model will automatically have the Siege Specialist skill at no points cost. This skill does not count toward their maximum number of skills.

- Iron Warrior forces make extensive use of Obliterators, with whom they have a special association. The normal 0-1 unit limitation in the main list does not apply to them.

- The Iron Warriors are characterised by their heavy equipment and may include an extra Heavy Support selection in return for two Fast Attack selections. Using the standard force organisation chart they may therefore have four Heavy Support selections and one Fast Attack selection.

- Large amounts of artillery are needed for sieges so the Iron Warriors have learned to capture and re-construct Imperial equipment for the job. An Iron Warriors army can include up to one Basilisk (see Codex: Imperial Guard) and up to one Vindicator (see Codex: Space Marines) as Heavy Support Choices. The Basilisk remains BS3 and may be upgraded to fire indirectly. The Vindicator's storm bolter is replaced by a pintle combi-bolter. The only vehicle upgrades allowed are those specified in this book.

- The Iron Warriors are technically gifted and have the equipment to accompany their skills. Iron Warriors may therefore use Servo Arms.

Servo Arm – 30 pts

In the Imperium, servo arms are the tools of Techmarines. In the Iron Warriors servo arms are used primarily as weapons but still facilitate the repair of immobilised vehicles. A model with a servo arm can attempt to repair an immobilised vehicle it is in base contact with at the start of the Chaos turn. Roll a D6; on a 6 the vehicle is repaired and may move normally. If used in close combat the bearer can make one additional attack each round with the arm, which counts as a power fist used with the bearer's Weapon Skill.

Night Lords

Originating on a world of perpetual night under the leadership of the Night Haunter, a vigilante who ruled by fear it is unsurprising that the Night Lords are experts in the art of terror. The Emperor was on the verge of dealing with the Night Lords' excesses when the Heresy began. The Night Lords established a brutal reputation on the eastern fringes, attacking by surprise and showing absolutely no mercy to their unfortunate victims. Even the assassination of Night Haunter himself could not stop them. The catalogue of atrocities they have perpetuated and continue to perpetuate are their way of sapping their enemies' will to resist.

Many weak, frightened planetary governors have capitulated rather than face the wrath of the Night Lords; none has ever been spared as a consequence.

Night Lord tactics are based on terror. No Legion is as careful as them in severing enemy communications and making visible examples of those who dare to oppose them. Darkness is their ally and they ruthlessly use their innate abilities to give themselves an advantage over their enemies. Aggressive patrolling and surprise raids are their stock in trade, they will patiently win a hundred small victories in order to achieve their objectives rather than pinning everything on one big battle.

- Because the Night Lords do not worship the Chaos Powers as gods they are reluctant to enter into Daemonic pacts so there are few Daemons in their armies. Chaos Furies are often enslaved by Raptor Cults, however, and so may be included. Daemon Princes and Possessed Chaos Space Marines are further exceptions as they are essentially Night Lords with Daemonic abilities.

- Marked models may only bear the Mark of Chaos Undivided. Vehicles may not be dedicated to any of the Chaos Gods in particular.

- All Night Lord Chaos Space Marines have the Night Vision Veteran skill at no cost in points and have sole rights to the Stealth Adept skill. The Night Sight skill does not count toward their maximum number of skills.

- The Night Lords are skilled raiders and make excellent use of both Chaos Space Marine Bikes and Raptors. To reflect this, they may use an additional Fast Attack selection in return for two less Heavy Support selections. Using the standard force organisation chart they may therefore have one Heavy Support selection and four Fast Attack selections.

- Night Lords forces make extensive use of Raptors. The normal 0-1 unit limitation in the main list does not apply to them.

Stealth Adept Skill 5/1 pts
The squad can maximise the benefits of any cover available, and therefore gains an extra +1 to their cover save. For example, a cover save of 5+ would count as a cover save of 4+. The squad still gets no cover save when in open ground. Models with a Bike, Steed, Daemonic Stature or Terminator Armour cannot use this skill.

Word Bearers

The Word Bearers are in many ways the most zealous of the Chaos Space Marine Legions. Before the Heresy, they and their Primarch, Lorgar, were fanatical devotees of the Imperial Cult. The Emperor wanted warriors, though, not disciples and criticised their behaviour. The Word Bearers took this rejection badly and doubtless encouraged by Horus came under the sway of the Chaos Gods, whose desire for worship exceeded that of the Emperor. The Word Bearers do not follow any one Chaos God but are dedicated to them all as a pantheon. Their dedication is demonstrated by supporting heretical cults and erecting cathedrals to the Chaos Gods on worlds that fall to them.

The tactics employed by the Word Bearers are influenced heavily by the Daemons they can call upon. They make frequent use of Daemons to shock and terrorise their enemies, seeing themselves as being higher in the grand order of Chaos than any Daemon, save perhaps the Greater Daemons. They have no compunctions about sending Daemons to their destruction.

The Word Bearers are the only Chaos Legion that still includes Chaplains in their ranks. Having abandoned the Imperial faith at the start of the Horus Heresy, Word Bearer Chaplains are now Dark Apostles of Chaos. When they lead the army, the Word Bearers are willing to make any sacrifice to achieve victory. The only way a Word Bearers advance can be stopped is by command of the Apostle or the death of every Word Bearer.

Word Bearers Chaos Space Marine forces are frequently unbalanced, sometimes omitting heavy armour completely, for example. This is because the Legion fights in accordance with the visions of the Apostles. The result can be tactics that border on prescience.

Forced conversion by indoctrination is a common fate for those conquered by their armies, often as a precursor to a short, brutal life as a labour slave building immense temples to the Chaos Gods. Their faith is a valuable commodity to the Chaos Gods and they have been rewarded with the service of hosts of Daemons to further their aims.

- The only Mark that may be assigned to models in a Word Bearers army is the Mark of Chaos Undivided.

- The Word Bearers may use any type of Daemon.

- Amongst the Word Bearers the most distinctive leaders are their Apostles; only the Word Bearers include Chaplains in their ranks and they are the zealots that drive the Legion onward. One Word Bearer Lord or Lieutenant can be designated as a Chaplain, or Dark Apostle, and must be equipped with an Accursed Crozius as testament to his origins. Any Chaplain may have the Demagogue ability (see opposite) to represent his firebrand oratory.

- Because of the large numbers of Daemon packs that the Word Bearers can call upon they may always include additional Troops choices on the force organisation chart to replace one each of Elites, Fast Attack and Heavy Support choices. Effectively this means they could have nine Troops selections in the same army although they would then only have two each of Elites, Fast Attack and Heavy Support.

- As with the other Undivided Legions, Veterans are a major feature of Word Bearer armies with all skills being utilised.

Accursed Crozius (Daemon Weapon)   **40 pts**

During the Horus Heresy most of the Chaplains of the Traitor Legions resisted the taint of Chaos and were murdered by their brethren. The Chaplains of the Word Bearer Legion embraced Chaos willingly though and as an act of faith ritually desecrated their once sacred weapons. These cursed crozius have a powerful effect as talismans of Chaos, proving that even the most pious of the Emperor's followers can be turned to the Path of Damnation.

The Accursed Crozius is a power weapon that is available only to Word Bearer models with the Mark of Chaos Undivided. Its wielder counts as having a Personal Icon of Chaos Undivided. Additionally, the bearer enjoys the protection of the Dark Gods and receives a 4+ Invulnerable save.

Demagogue Ability   **20 pts**

The Word Bearer is exceptionally well-versed in the counter-arguments to the Imperial creed. Moreover he is a skilled orator who is able to incite his brethren to a fanatical fervour. The orator, and all Chaos units apart from Daemons with a model within 6" of the orator will automatically pass any Morale checks they are required to take. This skill is available only to independent characters and does not count toward their maximum number of skills.

Black Legion

The Black Legion was originally known as the Luna Wolves, they were the Legion of Horus, greatest of the Primarchs and Warmaster of the Imperium, changing their name to the Sons of Horus in recognition of his victory in the Ullanor Crusade. When they were defeated in the Heresy, Abaddon the Despoiler rose to leadership and commanded that the Legion repaint their armour black to mirror their shame. From this time they have been known as the Black Legion.

They are mercurial in their allegiances to the Chaos Gods and regularly switch their support from one to another. They frequently allow themselves to be possessed by warp entities, secure in the knowledge they can free themselves when circumstances dictate. Under Abaddon's command they have re-established their reputation and are at the forefront of every Black Crusade.

The Black Legion is in many ways the basis for Codex: Chaos Space Marines. It is without doubt the most diverse Legion and makes use of all the troops and equipment available to Chaos Space Marine armies. At any given time, at least one of their Companies will probably be aligned with each of the major powers but not in any lasting way. They are always free to use any options in the list. Thus units of Black Legion Berzerkers bearing the Mark of Khorne will march side by side with Black Legion Sorcerers of Tzeentch under the command of a Black Legion Lord with the Mark of Chaos Undivided. Individual companies can be very different from one another, emphasising in some cases heavy armour, in others massed daemons. The preferences and history of the commanding Chaos Lord are the only real arbiter of their make-up.

Tactically, the Black Legion varies from company to company but all are guided by the implacable will of Abaddon the Despoiler so follow the same general approach. The Legion favours close action over ranged combat and will normally seek to apply constant pressure on the enemy. This is achieved by means of sharp but limited assaults to disrupt the enemy and capture positions which can be used for fire support. This in turn keeps the pressure on while a new series of assaults are prepared. The time-lag between attacks gradually declines giving the enemy less time to respond. The Black Legion Commander will wait at the head of his Chosen for the pressure to tell before launching a final, devastating assault in which teleporting Terminators often feature. Hordes of Daemons are frequently used for frontal attacks to pin the enemy and the Legion is adept at ensuring that the right specialists are used for each mission.

Abaddon the Despoiler

Abaddon is the Despoiler, the Arch-Fiend whose name has become a tenfold curse for the ten thousand years of terror he has rained upon the galaxy he once helped to conquer in the name of the Emperor.

As a Captain in the Lunar Wolves, Abaddon was the chosen of Horus and was rumoured even to be his clone son. His dedication to Horus was complete and the effect on him of his Primarch's death at the hands of the Emperor was shattering. Taking the Talon of Horus as his Icon he began down the road to vengeance. He reunified the Sons of Horus under his command renaming them the Black Legion and made pacts with the Infernal powers for their aid. He took the daemon sword Drach'nyen from its crypt and with its power at his disposal lead a succession of Black Crusades out of the Eye of Terror. Abaddon built his reputation with a series of acts of almost suicidal bravery, personally leading attacks into the most heavily defended positions and miraculously prevailing. Gradually it became accepted that the Gods of Chaos themselves had shaped his destiny and that Abaddon was the one who would lead the traitor legions to redemption through victory.

Worlds have burned as his sacrifice to the Gods of Chaos. His followers know he will brook no failure and follow him without question. No other Warmaster can rival his power and only he has ever been able to command the obedience of all nine Traitor Legions. He is the personification of the power of Chaos, the ultimate prodigal son whose return will bring the apocalypse.

	Points	WS	BS	S	T	W	I	A	Ld	Sv
Abaddon	255	6	5	4	4(5)	3	5	4(+1)	10	2+

A Chaos Space Marine army of 2,000 points or more may be led by Abaddon. If you take him then he counts as the Chaos Lord choice for the army. He must be used exactly as described below and may not be given extra equipment from the Chaos Armoury.

Wargear and Gifts: Talon of Horus (a master-crafted lightning claw with integral combi-bolter and which counts as a Personal Icon), Daemon Sword Drach'nyen, Chaos Terminator armour, Demagogue (see page 43), Daemonic Rune, Spiky bits.

SPECIAL RULES

Daemon Sword Drach'nyen: This arcane blade contains the bound essence of Drach'nyen, a writhing warp entity that can rend reality apart. The sword makes one attack per turn, with no re-rolls. Any hit inflicted ignores armour saves and kills the victim outright. Vehicles struck by the blade are penetrated automatically.

Mark of Chaos Ascendant: Abaddon has attained the favour of each of the Chaos powers in turn, and has proved the equal of his mentor Horus in that he has resisted becoming the pawn of any individual patron. Over the millennia Abaddon has melded the Marks of Chaos granted to him, and now bears a unique Mark that combines all of the gifts granted to him. The Mark of Chaos Ascendant is counted as a Mark of Chaos Undivided for troop selection purposes. The other benefits are included in his profile. Abaddon is Fearless and therefore assumed to automatically pass all Morale checks and Pinning tests he is called upon to make.

Chaos Terminator Armour: Abaddon's Terminator armour is adorned with various archaic devices, runes and fetishes that he has attained over the millennia. The armour has the abilities of normal Terminator armour but the 'Crux Terminatus' invulnerable save is increased to 4+. The armour will also nullify any psychic power used against Abaddon, or that includes him in its area of effect, on a D6 roll of 4+. In addition, Abaddon's Terminator armour incorporates a Daemonic Rune gifted to him by the Daemon-oracle of Asellus Tertius.

Independent Character: Unless accompanied by a Retinue, Abaddon follows the Independent Character special rules in the Warhammer 40,000 rulebook.

Retinue: Abaddon may be accompanied by a bodyguard of his finest warriors. See the Chosen entry in the army list for details.

> *"Horus was weak. Horus was a fool. He had the whole galaxy within his grasp and he let it slip away."*

THE BOOK OF KHORNE

THE BLOOD GOD

When the tribes of Man first travelled abroad upon the lands and seas of ancient Terra, when first they met their distant kin, their first words were not of peace and brotherly love. They were of anger, hatred and rage. This is the tragedy and saddest irony of Mankind; that in a universe poised to destroy him at every turn, in a world where his only friend is his brother; Mankind is as likely to turn his weapon upon his fellow man as upon his enemy.

Khorne is the manifestation of this violent, irrational aspect of human nature. He is the living embodiment of every hate-fuelled blow, every brutal killing, every pointless murder ever committed in the long, sad history of the Human race.

The Blood God sits upon a brass throne atop a mountain of skulls. The remains are those of his victims and his champions both, for he cares not whose blood is shed in his name. The skull mount forms an island amidst a vast ocean of blood: the living sacrificial essence of every victim of violent death throughout the ages.

Khorne is generally the dominant Chaos god, for he draws on the rawest, most elemental forces of human nature. His armies heave with those ensnared by notions of courage, honour, martial pride and revenge: all such concepts lead ultimately to the base of the Blood God's throne.

On every one of the million and more worlds that make up the Imperium there exist bodies of armed men. From the smallest garrison to the most populous fortress-world guarding an entire sector, warriors gather and train. Amidst these groups grow elite cadres, warrior-cults for whom martial pride and honour is all. Honour may give these men strength on the field of battle, but against Khorne it will prove their undoing, for pride becomes conceit in the Realm of Chaos, and from conceit it is but a short step to tyranny.

The Imperium of Man is driven by war. Upon thousands of worlds, a billion warriors strive for nothing more than slaughter. Amidst bloodshed on such a scale Khorne finds his followers, for when war has stripped a man of all decency, compassion and humanity, then his soul is open wide to the howling, hate-driven oaths of the Blood God.

The antithesis of Khorne is Slaanesh. The Blood God rails against his rival's decadence and love of luxury. Where a follower of Khorne conquers through the application of crude, brutal force, a champion of Slaanesh delights in each delicate stroke of the blade, only releasing his victims from his attentions when they are wasted and used. Khorne also finds an opposite in Tzeentch, the Lord of Sorcery, whose elaborate scheming and use of magic he scorns as cowardly.

The Mark of Khorne

The Mark of Khorne can be bestowed upon an Independent Character for +10 pts or to every model in a unit for +5 points per model. A model with the Mark of Khorne fights in a blood-crazed frenzy, preferring to fight hand-to-hand than at range. These Berzerkers despise sorcery, needing no more than their ferocity and a good chainaxe to defeat their enemies. Models with the Mark of Khorne may never have the Sorcerer ability and can never select from the Psychic Abilities & Equipment section of the Armoury.

Models with the Mark of Khorne are all gifted with Blood Frenzy.

Blood Frenzy

Models with Blood Frenzy:

- Gain +1 Attack.
- Are Fearless.
- Must charge if there are any enemy (including vehicles or creatures they cannot hurt) in range at the start of the Assault phase.
- At the start of their Movement phase, roll a D6 for each unit or independent character suffering from Blood Frenzy (do not roll for vehicles, Dreadnoughts, bikes or models using Daemonic Flight, Daemonic Steed or Daemonic Speed) to see if they are gripped so strongly by the frenzy that they must rush towards the enemy. On a 1 or 2 they advance a normal move +D6" towards the nearest enemy instead of moving normally. If mounted in a transport they will disembark before moving.
- Units that have made a Blood Frenzy move may not fire in the Shooting phase.

- If victorious in an assault they must sweeping advance unless any models are equipped with Terminator armour or they won due to 'moral high ground'.
- A character with Blood Frenzy may not join a unit without it and a character without Blood Frenzy may not join a unit with it simply because those subject to Blood Frenzy cannot give or receive cogent commands.

Weaponry of the Followers of Khorne

The following weapon upgrades are available to units with the Mark of Khorne:

Chosen, Chaos Space Marines, Possessed Chaos Space Marines and Chaos Biker units with the Mark of Khorne may upgrade their close combat weapons to Khornate chainaxes for +1 point per model. Models in power armour cannot upgrade their ranged weaponry other than to replace a bolt pistol with a plasma pistol at the normal cost.

Independent characters and Aspiring Champions may select from the armoury as normal.

Vehicles of Khornre

A vehicle dedicated to Khorne has the Destroyer ability. This costs +25 pts. A Defiler may not be given this upgrade.

Destroyer

The vehicle is equipped with all manner of spikes, slicing blades, scythed wheels, grabbing claws and torture implements.

If given to a Dreadnought it may re-roll one close combat miss in each round of close combat and when rolling for Fire Frenzy will enter Blood Rage on a 1 or 2.

If given to a tank, then during tank shock each enemy forced to move takes a wound on 4+ with normal saves allowed.

Armoury of Khorne

The following items are added to the main Armoury but can only be selected by models with the Mark of Khorne. The normal restrictions by category of item stated in the main Armoury section apply. Items marked with * can be used by models in Terminator armour.

Axe of Khorne*	.20/15 points
Banner of Rage*	.20 points
Berserker Glaive* (Daemon weapon)	40 points
Collar of Khorne*	.5 points
Feel no Pain*	.10/5 points
Juggernaut of Khorne	.35 points
Khornate Chainaxe	.3/1 points
Rage of Khorne	.15 points
Talisman of Burning Blood	.10/5 points

Axe of Khorne

The Axe of Khorne is imbued with the insatiable bloodlust of Khorne. Hits from the Axe of Khorne ignore armour saves. In addition, any to hit roll of 6 allows the model to make an additional attack. As long as you keep rolling 6s you can keep making additional attacks.

Banner of Rage

The Banner of Rage contains the bound souls of the most bloodthirsty of Khorne's servants. It radiates palpable waves of anger and lust for slaughter which beat upon the minds of those near it, driving them into a killing frenzy. As well as functioning as an Icon for Daemon Summoning purposes, the banner may unleash its special power once per battle in any Assault phase (including your opponent's). Any models in the same unit as the model bearing the Banner get +1 Attack.

Collar of Khorne

The Collar of Khorne is a talisman forged in the heat of Khorne's rage at the very foot of the Blood God's throne of brass. The collar is able to suck the energy from the Warp from around it, fortifying the bearer against psychic onslaughts.

As a result, force weapons lose their special ability to kill the bearer outright, and psychic abilities that target the wearer or include him in their area of effect are nullified and will not work on a D6 roll of 2+.

Berserker Glaive

The bearer of the Berserker Glaive carries a weapon he must constantly struggle for dominion over. The blade contains the bound essence of a Bloodletter driven to the depths of rage by its captivity. Although the Glaive is a devastating weapon, it has no compunction over whose life is taken.

The Berserker Glaive is a two-handed power weapon, which can only be carried by an independent character. The bearer cannot then join another unit, be accompanied by Followers or ride a Steed. In effect the model is treated as a unit in his own right rather than a character. He can therefore be picked out by enemy fire. Each turn, Blood Frenzy automatically grips the bearer without having to roll the dice. The Glaive confers a 4+ Invulnerable save on the bearer and doubles the basic number of attacks on his profile. The bearer must always sweeping advance when victorious in close combat (unless wearing Terminator armour). See the full rules for Daemon weapons on page 13.

Feel no Pain

Some followers of Khorne are able to focus their rage to the point that nothing except their total obliteration will stop their rampage. If they lose a wound' roll a dice; on a 3 or less the wound is taken as normal, on a 4 or more the wound is ignored and the model continues fighting. This ability cannot be used against weapons whose strength is at least twice the Toughness of the model being hit or against close combat weapons that allow no save.

Juggernaut of Khorne

Steed. The Juggernaut is a massive entity, part daemon and part brass-etched machine which is favoured as a mount by Champions of Khorne. Its sheer bulk confers the Daemonic Strength and Daemonic Essence abilities on its rider, in addition its ability to trample enemies underfoot confers the Daemonic Mutation ability.

Khornate Chainaxe

Blows struck by a Khornate Chainaxe are so powerful that they can penetrate virtually any armour. The best armour save possible against its attacks is 4+. Note that the first points cost is applicable to Independent Characters, the second to members of units.

Rage of Khorne

The Champion is so consumed by the need for battle that its rage builds and builds until it can be released in the first frenzy of close combat. The model gets +D3 extra attacks for charging instead of the normal +1.

Talisman of Burning Blood

When testing for Blood Frenzy, any model bearing this talisman, together with any unit bearing the Mark of Khorne that they are part of or have joined, rolls two dice rather than one to see if they enter Blood Frenzy. If either is a 1 or 2 they advance as described in the Blood Frenzy rule.

The World Eaters

The disciples of Khorne, the World Eaters, are utterly dedicated to his murderous ideals. They fight only to heap skulls at the base of their master's throne. To kill and to maim are the only tenets of their faith, and there are none more dedicated to this belief than the Berserkers of Khorne.

A World Eaters force may consist of a single champion and a small band of followers or it may contain hundreds of frothing madmen, but in either case its members are frenzied hand-to-hand fighters. When the enemy are defeated, the World Eaters are as likely to turn upon each other as they are to seek out new foes.

Playing a World Eaters army

If you want to use a pure World Eaters army you must adhere to the following limitations.

- All characters and units must have the Mark of Khorne. Characters and units that cannot have the Mark cannot be used.
- The only Daemons that can be used are those belonging to Khorne.
- Vehicles may only be dedicated to Khorne, although they may be undedicated.
- Any Favoured unit allowed Aspiring Champions may upgrade one model to an Aspiring Champion for free.
- Favoured Daemon Packs or Daemonic Beasts units may add +1 to their Summoning roll.

Khârn the Betrayer

Even before the Horus Heresy, Khârn of the World Eaters Legion was known as a bloodthirsty and unstable warrior. During the Heresy he became a legend, his uncompromising ferocity knew no equal and he was in the forefront of every attack on the Emperor's Palace. Khârn fell atop a mound of his victims in one of the breaches just as Horus was defeated. Unusually the World Eaters were drawn to carry his body away with them although they were sure he was dead. His revival was perceived as the blessing of Khorne for a valued servant. Since this time Khârn has cut his way through the bloodiest wars known with no wound to match the one he received on Terra.

Khârn earned his title as 'The Betrayer' when the World Eaters battled the Emperor's Children on Skalathrax. Seeing his brothers pause as the long night came to Skalathrax, freezing everything not under shelter, Khârn seized a flamer and forced them to fight by burning down the shelters. Khârn then stalked through the streets of Skalathrax's black cities uncompromisingly taking skulls for the Skull Throne of Khorne from both sides.

Khârn's actions that long night split the World Eaters Legion into small self-sufficient warbands and only the most committed and/or psychotic amongst them would ever fight alongside Khârn again. Khârn cares not; he is a tireless destroyer whose single, overwhelming need is to slay in Khorne's name.

	Points	WS	BS	S	T	W	I	A	Ld	Sv
Khârn	180	7	5	4	4	4	5	5	10	2+

A Chaos Space Marine army may include Khârn as long as it also includes at least one squad bearing the Mark of Khorne. If you decide to take him then he counts as one of the HQ choices for the army. He must be used exactly as described below and may not be given extra equipment from the Chaos Armoury.

Wargear and Gifts: Plasma pistol, frag & krak grenades, Daemonic armour, Gorechild. Mark of Khorne (bonus included above), Collar of Khorne, Talisman of Burning Blood, Rage of Khorne and Daemonic Rune.

SPECIAL RULES

Gorechild: Khârn's huge and ancient chain-axe, Gorechild, is an artefact from the Great Crusade. Gorechild's jagged whirring teeth were torn from the jaws of mica-dragons on Luther Mcintyre, its haft is forged of adamantium, and its head is a full three spans across. Khârn is so skilled with Gorechild that in hand-to-hand combat the enemy's WS is ignored and all his close combat attacks always hit on a roll of 2+. This aside, Gorechild is treated as a normal power weapon.

The Betrayer: Khârn may attack anyone nearby in his berserk fury, friend or foe alike! To represent this, any of Khârn's to hit dice that roll a 1 will count as having hit his own side. Resolve the hits on the closest single friendly unit or independent character within 6" of Khârn as if they were hit by the enemy, but using Khârn's weapons and profile. Obviously, it makes sense for the Chaos player to keep Khârn as far away from models on his own side as possible!

Independent Character: Khârn is an independent character and follows all the independent character special rules as given in the Warhammer 40,000 rulebook.

> *"Kill! Maim! Burn! Kill! Maim! Burn! Kill! Maim! Burn! Kill! Maim! Burn! Kill! Maim! Burn! Kill! Maim! Burn! Kill! Maim! Burn!"*
>
> Khârn of the World Eaters

Death is the only constant in the realm of Man, and with death comes decay. Nurgle is the embodiment of disease and deterioration, the elemental forces that hold in check the energies of progress and evolution. There exists within every mortal the desire to let all around him rot, and to exult in the processes of disease and decomposition.

Nurgle empowers those who would see every accomplishment of Mankind reduced to mouldering ruin. He is the Lord of Decay, and his servants spread disease and contagion throughout the mortal realm in the name of their festering master.

Yet Nurgle's power embodies, by its very nature, the notion of the eternal cycle of life. Decay is inevitable, but so too is rebirth. The form that rebirth may take is, of course, rarely the ideal and if Nurgle has his way then it will take a form loathsome to Man.

Nurgle's appearance is the most abhorrent of the Chaos gods. His bloated body is home to every form of corruption imaginable, and his skin is covered in weeping sores. Foul Nurglings cavort amongst Nurgle's exposed organs, giggling with insane delight at the latest pestilence inflicted upon Mankind by their master.

Nurgle's followers suffer under the burden of his 'gifts' as much as they benefit from them. These gifts often take the form of repulsive diseases and hideous deformations which, while useful in spreading Nurgle's contagions, may often lead to the death of the carrier. The servants of Nurgle cry out to him to rid them of the gifts they so blatantly invited when they turned to worship him, and he takes great sport in prolonging their suffering through the granting of yet more of his marks.

Nurgle's power within the pantheon of the Chaos gods is inextricably linked to his workings in the mortal realm. When disease and pestilence are rife, then the Lord of Decay's influence is at its height. The very nature of Nurgle's power is such that it will inevitably consume all of its victims and leave few survivors to perpetuate the contagion. At this point the plague god's might wanes and his plans falter. But one thing is certain: the plague is never truly eradicated, and its spores are often spread far and wide before exploding into yet another epidemic, when once again Nurgle's legions are swelled with the grotesque living dead.

The only power that can oppose deterioration and decay are those represented by Tzeentch: change and evolution. The two gods are engaged in a galaxy-wide struggle of opposing forces, and whichever wins, the inhabitants of the material realms will be the ones who pay the highest price.

The Mark of Nurgle

The Mark of Nurgle can be bought for an independent character at +10 pts or for all members of a unit at +5 points per model. A model with the Mark of Nurgle is a living host for all manner of poxes and infections, which it spreads for the greater glory of the Lord of Decay. Horrific to behold and almost impossible to kill, Plague Marines are a blight on all life. Models with the Mark of Nurgle are Fearless and gifted with Daemonic Resilience.

No unit with the Mark of Nurgle may carry any of the following weapons: lascannon, autocannon, missile launcher or heavy bolter.

The Primarch of the Death Guard, Mortarion, trained his warriors to fight on foot relying on their bolters to cut down their enemies. Loyal to his teachings down the centuries Plague Marines have learned to use their bolters in close combat, a feat aided by their ability to absorb the ferocious recoil with their diseased bulk. All models with the Mark of Nurgle have True Grit to reflect this.

True Grit

Bolters have a 'pistol grip' which means they can be fired with a single hand. This takes considerable practice and skill and is not normally encouraged. Models with True Grit, however, have learned how to use their bolters in this manner. In game terms, this means that they may count their bolter as a bolt pistol in close combat and will therefore be allowed to roll an extra Attack dice if they have been equipped with a second pistol or close combat weapon. However, a model using their bolter in this manner may not receive the attack bonus for charging, as a bolter is too unwieldy to be fired with one hand while simultaneously hurling yourself at the enemy.

Vehicles of Nurgle

A vehicle dedicated to Nurgle has the Plague Carrier ability. This costs +15 points.

Plague Carrier

The vehicle is equipped with smouldering censers which release billowing clouds of sickly smoke in its wake and has the same effect as the Nurgle gift Nurgle's Rot.

The Gifts of Nurgle

The following items are added to the main Armoury but can only be selected by models with the Mark of Nurgle. The normal restrictions by category of item stated in the main Armoury section apply. Items marked with * can be used by models in Terminator armour.

Blight Grenades	.25 points
Manreaper* (Daemon Weapon)	.25 points
Minor Psychic Power*	.10 points
Nurgle's Rot*	.5 points
Nurgling Infestation*	.20 points
Pandemic Staff* (Daemon Weapon)	.25 points
Plague Banner*	.50 points
Plague Sword*	.25/15 points

Blight Grenades

These are made from the shrunken heads of those killed by Father Nurgle's favourite plagues. Any enemy unit charged by one or more models with blight grenades suffers a -1 to hit modifier in the ensuing close combat round.

Manreaper

This rusted and corrupted blade has been dipped in the filth seeping from the very throne of Nurgle, and in so doing absorbed the essence of one of the Daemons that cavort there.

The Manreaper is a two-handed power weapon in the shape of a scythe. With each sweep the long blade can cut through several enemies. The bearer gets +D6 extra attacks to reflect this. If the Manreaper's wielder directs his attacks at a single enemy model he will receive only one bonus Attack as the weapon is too long and unwieldy to be easily readied for further blows.

Nurgle Minor Psychic Power

The model may make a single roll on the Nurgle Minor Psychic Power table. Duplicate powers are re-rolled, but rolls of 1 are not.

Nurgling Infestation

Champions of Nurgle are frequently accompanied by swarms of Nurglings eager to feed off the flakes of dead and diseased flesh they trail behind them. If their host is in close combat the Nurglings will attack fiercely providing their host with an extra D6 Strength 3 attacks at Initiative 3 (exactly as if the attacks were being made by a Nurglings base) against enemies in base contact. The Nurglings should be modelled on the host's base and person.

Nurgle's Rot

At the end of the Chaos Shooting phase, any model that is within 6" of at least one model with Nurgle's Rot may be affected by the miasma of disease and pestilence exuding from them. Roll a D6 for each affected model, and on a roll of a 6 it takes a wound. Armour and Invulnerable saves may be taken, but not cover saves. Models with the Mark of Nurgle, their followers, and all Daemon Packs, Possessed, Daemon Beasts and Greater Daemons are immune.

Pandemic Staff

The Pandemic Staff acts as a Vessel for Grandfather Nurgle's favourite contagions when they are carried from the Warp into the real universe.

The Pandemic Staff is a normal close combat weapon. Its bearer may use it in the Shooting phase instead of firing another weapon. An enemy unit within 12" can be targeted. Test to hit every model in the target unit on a roll of 4+. Hits are resolved at Strength 3 and normal saving throws apply.

Plague Sword

The Plague Sword drips with venomous pus. No armour saves are allowed against its blows and in addition roll a D6 for each model wounded by it but not killed. On a roll of 4+ it will be killed outright no matter how many wounds they have.

Plague Banner

The Plague Banner is a hideous fabrication of rotting hides which flap in a pestilent wind. Not only can it function like a normal Icon but, in addition, a powerful curse is held in the standard that can be released once per battle in the owner's Shooting phase. Any one enemy unit with a model within 6" of the banner will take D6 wounds just as shooting with no armour or cover saves possible.

The Death Guard

Servants of Nurgle, the Death Guard fight only to spread contagion and death throughout the galaxy. These once proud Space Marines have now been reduced to pestilent, disease-infested killers.

The Death Guard consist largely of Plague Marines; creatures so vile they have given their entire existence to spreading Nurgle's Rot amongst the living. Those infected with the rot meet a painful death, their bodies reduced to a mass of weeping sores and pestilent weals. Death is no release for these wretches, who find themselves reborn into the service of Grandfather Nurgle, to whom their cries for relief from the ever-present plague are like the clamouring of loving children.

Playing a Death Guard army

If you want to use a pure Death Guard army you must adhere to the following limitations.

- All characters and units must have the Mark of Nurgle. Characters or units that cannot have the Mark cannot be used.
- The only Daemons that can be used are those of Nurgle.
- Vehicles may only be dedicated to Nurgle although they may be undedicated.
- The Death Guard are primarily infantry-based, and lack the specialised Fast Attack choices available to other Chaos forces. As a result, the limited number of Rhinos available to them are dedicated to this role. To reflect this lack in game terms, only two Plague Marine squads with Rhinos may be counted as Troops choices; all others are counted as Fast Attack choices instead.
- Favoured Daemon Packs may add +1 to their Summoning roll.
- Any favoured unit allowed Aspiring Champions may upgrade one model to an Aspiring Champion for free.

Nurgle Minor Psyker Powers

1. No usable power
Effect: The psyker's patron pays no heed to his prayers. The roll is wasted.

2. Nurgle's Dance
Phase: Own Shooting **Psychic Test?** Yes **Range:** 12"
Effect: The psyker calls to the enemy, inviting them to reveal themselves and join him in Nurgle's exuberant cavalcade. If the target unit or model is behind cover, it must make a Leadership test or lose the benefits of that cover for the remainder of the player turn.

3. Nausea
Phase: Enemy Shooting **Psychic Test?** Yes **Range:** 12"
Effect: The psyker is able to invoke nausea and disorientation amongst his foes. An enemy unit or independent character (but not a vehicle) within line of sight will be at -1 BS for this Shooting phase.

4. Affliction
Phase: Own Shooting **Psychic Test?** Yes **Range:** 12"
Effect: Calling upon Grandfather Nurgle, the psyker bestows a particularly choice contagion upon his foe. If successful, the psyker may target an independent character or unit (the owning player may nominate the target model within a unit, only one model is affected). If you roll over the victim's Toughness on a D6, or roll a 6 regardless of Toughness, then the target model takes a single wound with normal saves allowed.

5. Miasma of Pestilence
Phase: Own Shooting **Psychic Test?** Yes **Range:** 24"
Effect: The psyker calls forth clouds of pestilent flies and choking vapours, through which few enemies have the stomach to advance. Place the small blast marker at any point within the Psyker's line of sight and roll the Scatter Dice and a D6 to determine its final location (counting the target symbol as a hit). Any enemy unit with models under the template must make an immediate Morale check or fall back using the normal rules.

6. Aura of decay
Phase: Either Assault **Psychic Test?** Yes **Range:** 2"
Effect: The psyker surrounds himself in an aura of corruption and filth to such an extent that his enemies have difficulty engaging him. This power imposes a -1 Attack penalty (to a minimum of 1) on all enemy models in base contact. If the psychic test is failed then the modifier will apply to all friendly troops within 2" instead. The psyker may fight as normal in the phase this power is used.

Typhus

The Traveller, Herald of Nurgle, Host of the Destroyer Hive

When Mortarion, Primarch of the Death Guard, allied his Legion with the forces of Warmaster Horus he did not know the price that would be paid for his decision. One amongst the Death Guard knew full well though, his name was Typhon and he had been recruited like so many others into Mortarion's forces on the feral world of Barbarus where the Primarch had grown up. Barbarus was home not only to men but also to inhuman overlords that preyed upon them. Typhon had some of their blood in his veins for he was possessed of formidable latent psychic powers that made him especially valuable as a recruit. Even as Mortarion led his Death Guard on the Emperor's Great Crusade Typhon communed with the Dark Powers.

Typhon rose to the rank of Captain, commander of the battleship 'Terminus Est' and a full company of the Death Guard. When the Death Guard joined Horus it was he who slew the Death Guard's Navigators claiming their loyalty was still to the Emperor. It was he who promised Mortarion that his powers could lead the Death Guard through the Warp to Terra and it was he who led them to damnation, becalmed in the Warp, adrift and helpless.

When the Destroyer Plague came and the Death Guard for all their resilience were struck down Typhon received his reward from his true master, Nurgle, Lord of Decay. As the last member of the Death Guard fell, Typhon absorbed the full power of this most terrible plague. His body became a vessel for the ultimate corruption, his armour became a hive of pestilence. He was Typhon no longer, now he was Typhus, Herald of Nurgle and the host of the Destroyer Hive.

In the Eye of Terror Mortarion shaped his Daemon World to resemble Barbarus. Typhus was sickened by the sentimentality. His loyalty was to Nurgle and Nurgle waxed strong when mortals feared death. Taking his ship and his followers Typhus returned again and again to the mortal realm and the legend of the traveller, the Herald of Nurgle was born. The rewards granted him by Nurgle are testament to a score of blighted worlds and countless damned souls.

Destroyer Hive: Typhus' armour and body are host to a horrific plague that manifests as a swarm of insects that pour from the cracks and vents in his armour. When he charges into combat he counts as using frag and blight grenades. When he is charged Typhus and his retinue (if any) count as being in cover. In addition, the Nurgle's Rot carried by Typhus causes wounds on a 5+ instead of a 6.

Independent Character: Unless accompanied by a retinue Typhus is an independent character and all the rules regarding independent characters apply to him. See the Warhammer 40,000 rulebook for full details on independent characters.

	Points	WS	BS	S	T	W	I	A	Ld	Sv
Typhus	230	5	5	4	4(5)	4	5	3	10	2/5+

Typhus may be included in any Death Guard Chaos Space Marine army of at least 1,500 points as its Chaos Lord. He may be accompanied by a retinue of Chosen selected as normal but must otherwise be fielded exactly as specified.

Wargear and Gifts: Mark of Nurgle, Sorcerer, Daemonic Essence (+1 Wound, included in profile), Daemonic Visage, Nurgle's Rot, Nurgling Infestation, Terminator armour, Manreaper, Warp Talisman.

Psychic Abilities: Wind of Chaos; minor powers: Affliction and Miasma of Pestilence.

THE BOOK OF SLAANESH

THE PRINCE OF EXCESS

The hearts of mortals harbour the darkest of desires, and it is in Slaanesh that these desires find expression. Every culture imposes limits and standards on its peoples: Slaanesh is the manifestation of the desire to stretch these limits to breaking point, to exceed them, and to wallow in the act of violating every more of civilized society.

Slaanesh is the youngest of the Chaos gods, having burst into being some ten thousand years ago at the moment of the Fall of the Eldar. Eldar society had, over the course of many centuries, regressed to a state of hedonism and self-indulgence, where every whim could be satisfied in an instant. The very nature of the Eldar race made them susceptible to excess. In one cataclysmic climax, almost the entire race was destroyed and Slaanesh was born with such force that the Eye of Terror came into being and the Warp storms isolating Terra were driven away.

Slaanesh whispers to Man in many different voices; each whisper attuned to the most secret desires of the listener. Many desire perfection, whether in the intellect, the body or in ability, and Slaanesh will grant these individuals the power and drive to hone their desires to the utmost excellence. The artist will produce works beyond Human comprehension, the narcissist hones their visage so that other mortals are driven insane with desire, and the warrior develops such abilities that a casual gesture may decapitate the mightiest of foes. To the followers of Slaanesh, the material world is a riot of colour, sound and sensation. However, their senses soon become accustomed to these levels of stimulation and they are driven to extremes in search of the slightest fulfilment.

The followers of Slaanesh often exhibit the utmost physical perfection to the naked eye, and on the exterior it may be true that no mortal is capable of such beauty. But the soul of each follower screams in eternal torment, as the gifts bestowed by the Prince of Chaos are purchased at a price as high as that demanded by any other Chaos god: eternal damnation.

Slaanesh may appear as male, female, hermaphrodite or androgynous. Whichever form he takes, his physical beauty is such that no mortal may look upon him and resist the urge to submit. Slaanesh is the rival of Khorne, who he sees as crude and unsophisticated. The Prince of Chaos does not have the resources to seriously challenge the Blood God: the very nature of his power is such that it will ultimately expend itself long before Khorne's hordes have satisfied their bloodlust.

The Mark of Slaanesh

The Mark of Slaanesh can be bestowed upon an independent character at +10 points or to all members of a unit at a cost of +5 points per model. A model with the Mark of Slaanesh is addicted to sensation of all sorts and craves new and more extreme pleasures. Their excesses are made easier by a supernatural glamour that cloaks them, unnerving and disturbing their adversaries.

Models with the Mark of Slaanesh are Fearless and have the Warp Scream special ability.

Warp Scream

Peculiar to the followers of Slaanesh they can emit a piercing scream, which blurs the barriers between real space and the warp. This has a disorientating effect on their enemies whose Initiative is reduced by 1 (to a minimum of 1) in any turn in which they are attempting to attack a model with this ability in close combat.

Chosen, Chaos Space Marines, Chaos Havocs and Chaos Space Marine Bikers with the Mark of Slaanesh can replace their normal weapons with sonic weaponry as follows:

- replace a combi-bolter or twin-linked bolter with a sonic blaster at +2 pts, or replace a bolter with a sonic blaster at +5 points.
- replace an autocannon or reaper autocannon with a blastmaster at no extra cost.
- replace a meltagun with a doom siren, bolt pistol and close combat weapon at no cost. If mounted on a bike the model will have either the bolt pistol or the close combat weapon.

Independent characters and Aspiring Champions may select equipment from the Armoury as normal.

Vehicles of Slaanesh

A vehicle dedicated to Slaanesh has the Warp Amp ability. This costs +20 points.

Warp Amp

The vehicle is equipped with a device designed to amplify emotions and sensations by projecting resonant warp energies from rune-encrusted horns and pipes that sprout from the vehicle. Enemy within 12" are at -1 Ld, at -2 Ld within 6" or at -3 Ld in contact. Note that if performing a tank shock the Warp Amp and Blasphemous Rune abilities are cumulative. Count the nearest Warp Amp equipped vehicle only.

Armoury of Slaanesh

The following items are added to the main Armoury but can only be selected by models with the Mark of Slaanesh. The normal restrictions by category of item stated in the main armoury section apply. Items marked with a * can be used by models in Terminator armour.

Allure of Slaanesh	.25 points
Aura of Acquiescence*	.10 points
Combat Drugs*	.25 points
Doom Siren*	.10 points
Lash of Torment* (Daemon weapon)	.25 points
Minor Psychic Power*	.10 points
Needle of Desire* (Daemon weapon)	.25 points
Rapturous Standard*	.50 points
Sonic Blaster*	.5 points
Steed of Slaanesh	.25 points

Allure of Slaanesh

During the Shooting phase, instead of firing a weapon the Champion projects a siren song up to 12" at a single enemy independent character or unit that is not in close combat. Make a Leadership test for the model or unit affected. If they fail they must immediately move D6" toward the model, stopping 1" short of any Chaos models they encounter and ignoring difficult terrain penalties.

Aura of Acquiescence

Champions with this gift are wrapped in the glamour of Slaanesh. Such is their magnetism that their enemies subjugate their own survival instinct to the will of the Champion even if their cause is hopeless. If an enemy unit fights in close combat against a model with the Aura of Acquiescence and loses they do not take a Morale check and remain in combat.

Combat Drugs

Slaanesh champions have access to a wide variety of combat drugs, each produced from renderings of sentient creatures. They may be taken at the start of any Assault phase. When they are taken the Slaaneshi player can choose up to three abilities from the list below. The abilities rolled last for the duration of the Assault phase. Roll a D6 for each power chosen. If a double is rolled the character takes one wound that cannot be saved in any way. If a treble is rolled the character dies outright. If only a single power is chosen then the model cannot be harmed.

- If charging through difficult terrain the model may roll an additional dice when determining how far he moves.
- +1 Weapon Skill.
- +1 Strength.
- The model ignores the first unsaved wound taken in this Assault phase as long as it does not inflict 'instant death'.
- +1 Attack

Lash of Torment

The Lash is a whip that twists and coils with a mind of its own. Cruelly barbed hooks run along its length and its sinuous coils are warm yet unsettling to the touch. It thrives on the pain of its victims absorbing their fear and projecting it for the enjoyment (or terror) of all around. The lash is a one-handed power weapon which may be used at full effect in close combat even if the model wielding it is not in base contact but is within 2" of enemy in close combat with the unit he is with. A unit in close combat with the bearer of the Lash of Torment that loses one or more models to it that turn will be at -1 Leadership if they lose the combat and have to make a Morale check.

Slaanesh Minor Psychic Power

The model may make a single roll on the Slaanesh Minor Psychic Power table. Duplicate powers are re-rolled, but rolls of 1 are not.

Needle of Desire

The Needle of Desire is a long, slim double-pointed needle inscribed with runes within runes to a microscopic level. One half is embedded in the arm of the Champion bearing it where it absorbs the foul narcotics naturally synthesised by Champions of Slaanesh, only for it to be injected into enemies using the other end of the Needle.

The Needle of Desire always wounds on a 2+. Its venom will scourge a wounded enemy with extreme sensations from delirium to despair. The effect is so powerful that many victims will simply remain impaled on the needle and let the venom wash through them destroying them from the inside. Any model wounded and not killed must make a single Leadership test (regardless of how many times they were originally wounded) or take a further D3 wounds with no saves allowed. Note that the Needle is such a precise weapon that it does not ignore armour saves even if being used by a model with Daemonic Stature.

Rapturous Standard

The Rapturous Standard jingles with the sound of distant chimes and carries the scent of forbidden pleasure. As well as acting as a focus for summoning Daemons once per game (either in the Chaos player's phase or the enemy's) at the start of the Shooting phase its special power may be invoked. Any model within 6" becomes gains the Feel no Pain special ability (see the Wargear list in the Book of Khorne) for the remainder of the current player phase.

Steed of Slaanesh

Steed. These sinuous, graceful daemonic beasts are the preferred mounts of Champions of Slaanesh. Their long whip-like tongues confer the Daemonic Mutation ability and their writhing gait confers the Daemonic Speed ability.

The Emperor's Children

Once a Legion dedicated to perfection in all its pursuits, the Emperor's Children succumbed to the call of forbidden knowledge. Their drive for perfection was perverted to an obsession with excess, and the members of this Legion will stop at nothing to gratify their basest desires. Chaos Space Marines of the Emperor's Children make war into an art form; a riot of sounds, sights and sensations. Doom sirens wail and implements of torture slash as these followers of Slaanesh are driven to further extremes in order to stimulate their overloaded senses.

Playing an Emperor's Children army

If you want to use a pure Emperor's Children army you must adhere to the following limitations:

- All characters and units must have the Mark of Slaanesh. Characters or units that cannot have the Mark cannot be used.
- The only Daemons that can be used are those of Slaanesh.
- Vehicles may only be dedicated to Slaanesh although they may be undedicated.
- Any Favoured unit allowed Aspiring Champions may upgrade one model to an Aspiring Champion for free, and Favoured Daemon Packs may add +1 to their Summoning roll.
- Dreadnoughts with a Warp Amp may replace their twin-linked heavy bolters with twin-linked sonic blasters, their twin-linked autocannons with a blastmaster and their flamer with a doom siren. These adaptations do not cost any extra points but must be clearly depicted, all of them are optional and should only be used to represent a Dreadnought of the Emperor's Children Legion.
- Predators may upgrade an autocannon to a blastmaster for free, and may replace heavy bolters with sonic blasters for free.

Sonic Weaponry

Blastmaster

The Blastmaster is a weapon that focuses a throbbing bass note into an explosive crescendo. By varying the frequency of the blast the effect of the weapon can be altered to produce different effects.

Varied Frequency	Rng:36"	Str:5	AP:5	Assault 2, causes pinning
Single Frequency	Rng:36"	Str:8	AP:4	Heavy 1 blast

Doom Siren

A Doom Siren is a complex arrangement of pipes and tubes that magnifies the war cry of the Chaos Space Marine to a short range sonic attack. Instead of shooting with another weapon the wearer can make a shooting attack using the following profile:

Range: Template   Str 4   AP 5   Assault 1, no cover save

In close combat a model with a Doom Siren will always strike in Initiative sequence even if attacking enemy in cover as the waves of sonic energy confuse and repel them. Enemy who strike first regardless of initiative are unaffected.

Sonic Blaster

Unleashing waves of devastating harmonics, a sonic blaster literally rips its target apart. It has two profiles depending on whether it is used to unleash short bursts or a long discordant blast.

Range 24"   Str 4   AP 5   Assault 2 or Heavy 3.

Slaanesh Minor Psyker Powers

1. No usable power
Effect: The psyker's patron pays no heed to his prayers. The roll is wasted.

2. Fuelled by Pain
Phase: Either Assault Psychic Test? No Range: Self
Effect: Pain serves only to heighten the psyker's combat prowess. For every close combat attack that wounds the psyker, but is stopped by his Armour save, he may make an additional attack after all other attacks (including power fists) have been resolved but before combat results are determined. The psyker may fight as normal in the phase this power is used.

3. Siren
Phase: Enemy Shooting or Assault
Psychic Test? Yes Range: Self
Effect: The psyker assumes the appearance of an individual important, cherished or attractive to the enemy: one they would never harm in any way. This power may not be used if the psyker has joined a unit or is part of a unit. The psyker may not be targeted by shooting attacks or assaulted this game turn. This power cannot be attempted if the psyker is already in base-to-base contact with an enemy model.

4. Beam of Slaanesh
Phase: Enemy Shooting Psychic Test? Yes Range: 18"
Effect: The psyker unleashes a dazzling rainbow display that beguiles and disorientates his foe. The target model or unit must make a Leadership test or counts as having moved for the purposes of firing their weapons.

5. Touch of Slaanesh
Phase: Own Assault Psychic Test? Yes Range: Base contact
Effect: The psyker gifts each of his opponents with a delicate caress that renders them insensible and unable to avoid harm. All enemy models in base contact with the psyker suffer a -1 to their WS (to a minimum of 1) for the remainder of the phase. The psyker may fight as normal in the phase this power is used.

6. She Who Thirsts
Phase: Own Assault Psychic Test? Yes Range: Base contact
Effect: The psyker reaches out and attempts to pluck the very soul from his enemy, leaving little more than a withered husk in his wake. This is a sight that may put the bravest of troops to flight. If the psyker kills one or more enemy models in his own Assault phase the unit or units they belonged to will be at -1 Leadership if they lose the close combat and have to take a Morale check.

Lucius the Eternal
The Soulthief, Fulgrim's Champion, Scion of Chemos

Many millennia ago, Lucius was a Space Marine of the Emperor's Children Legion, following his Primarch Fulgrim across the galaxy in the name of the Emperor. He led his bodyguard of Assault Marines with such passion and skill that Fulgrim honoured him with the rank of Lord Commander. Forsaking all experience other than the art of combat, Lucius bore his many battle scars with pride, and over time, he began to equate pain with success. By the time the Emperor's Children were dispatched to challenge the rebellion of Horus, Lucius had cut deep patterns across his face, head and chest, linking the scars of centuries of battle in a maze of irregular patterns that distorted and deformed his features. His near-constant and self-inflicted flagellation was seen by his fellow Space Marines as a mark of commendable devotion and piety. The truth, however, was far darker.

Lucius continued to distinguish himself in the service of his Primarch as the Legion descended into Chaos worship. He fought with incredible speed and skill in the gladiatorial contests Fulgrim held when the Legion was unable to visit hell upon an unsuspecting world. He was almost invincible, a force of nature that could not be bested. Lucius remained undefeated until, when fighting the infamous Lord Commander Cyrius, he finally met his match. His agonising death was an experience of transcendent pleasure, but Slaanesh was loath to let such a promising protègè slip into the realm of the dead. Over the next few weeks, the artificer armour Cyrius wore began to warp and change. His hair fell out in clumps, and dark lines appeared under his flesh, slowly pushing through his skin as a maze of scar tissue. Soon, Lucius had emerged completely, and all that remained of his executioner was a screaming, writhing face, subsumed for eternity into Lucius's armour.

Thus it is that Lucius stalks the galaxy as an arrogant and sadistic slaughterer who can never truly be killed. Whoever slays him and takes even a moment of triumph from the act will find themselves transforming, slowly and painfully, into Lucius. The armour he wears writhes with the howling soul-remnants of many such unfortunates, affording him endless satisfaction. His skill with his chosen weapons, an ornate sabre and a daemon-infested whip, is puissant, and they have tasted the blood of champions and kings across the breadth of the galaxy. He leads his warhost with unnatural charisma and total confidence, welcoming death with as much passion as he inflicts it upon his foes.

A Chaos Space Marine army of may be led by Lucius the Eternal you decide to take him then he the HQ choices for the army. He must exactly as described below and may not be given extra equipment or psychic powers from the Chaos Armoury. He may be accompanied by a retinue of Chosen selected in the normal way.

1,500 points or more as its Chaos Lord. If counts as one of be used

Lucius counts as a psyker and always has the Fuelled by Pain minor psychic power (see page opposite). He can use no other psychic abilities.

SPECIAL RULES

Independent Character: Lucius is an independent character and all the rules for characters in the Warhammer 40,000 rulebook apply.

Martial pride: Although Lucius has little interest in slaughtering hapless mortals, when he is confronted by a worthy foe he fights with the speed and skill of an enraged daemon. Lucius's Attacks characteristic is raised to 5 when he is in base contact with an opponent whose Weapon Skill is five or more. It is lowered to 2 when all opponents in base contact have Weapon Skill 2 or less.

Armour of Shrieking Souls: The armour Lucius has worn for countless millennia is a baroque monstrosity writhing with the howling souls of those that have killed him over the aeons. This incredibly potent artefact of Chaos confers a 4+ Invulnerable save that may be taken instead of Lucius's normal Armour save. In addition, Lucius may discharge the cacophony generated by the tormented essences trapped within his armour; to represent this he counts as being equipped with a Doom Siren.

Lucius may never join a unit with a Mark other than that of Slaanesh.

	Pts	WS	BS	S	T	W	I	A	Ld	Sv
Lucius	196	5	5	5	4	3	5	3	10	3+

Wargear: Armour of Shrieking Souls, Mark of Slaanesh, Combat Drugs, Aura of Acquiescence, Power Sword, Lash of Torment, Daemonic Strength (already included in profile above).

Tzeentch weaves the threads that connect every action, plot and subtle intrigue in a galaxy-wide game of manipulation and subterfuge. At the end of each of these threads writhes the ensnared soul of a Human puppet; his servants and agents who believe they serve the Lord of Sorcery in mutually beneficial pacts. The truth is that Tzeentch's every action is planned with its ultimate goal as his own establishment as the pre-eminent power in the Warp. Of course, the very nature of the Lord of Entropy is such that, were he to attain this goal, he would still strive for turmoil and change.

Tzeentch exerts his influence in the mortal realm through subtle manipulations and devious ploys. His victims are sorcerers drawn by the promise of forbidden knowledge, politicians lured by the power to outmanoeuvre their opponents. His power is sorcery, and as all sorcery flows from the fount of the Warp, so too is Tzeentch the master of that twisted medium. Tzeentch embodies mutability and change, the drive to evolve and manipulate. This spirit is present in the essence of every living creature from the first division of cells within the womb to the ultimate craving for survival. It is in the hearts of those with the strongest desire to prevail that Tzeentch whispers his insidious promise; offering a means to life eternal to those unwilling to accept death and oblivion as inevitable.

The main rival of the Lord of Sorcery is Nurgle. Where Tzeentch seeks to build and evolve, the Lord of Decay desires only to break down and dissolve. On innumerable occasions Tzeentch's intricate plots have been foiled by Nurgle's malign influence, and the two gods' servants clash as often with each other as with their mutual enemies.

Despite Tzeentch's rivalry with Grandfather Nurgle, he is nonetheless the god with the most influence over the others. At times, the Chaos gods must unite and act in concert if their individual plans are to reach fruition, and it is always Tzeentch who brokers these alliances. However, Tzeentch never acts out of altruism, and it can be guaranteed that every time he moves to unite the powers of Chaos he does so ultimately with his own unfathomable goals in mind.

The Mark of Tzeentch

The Mark of Tzeentch can be bestowed upon a unit or character at a cost of +10 points per model. All such models are Fearless.

Independent Characters, Chosen and Possessed Chaos Space Marines

All models automatically have the Sorcerer ability without having to select the upgrade from their list entry. In addition they will automatically pass any Psychic Test they are required to take. The main list limits Chosen to one Sorcerer per unit, but if the unit has the Mark of Tzeentch, every model has the Sorcerer ability. Sorcerers may select from the Psychic Powers and Equipment section of the Armoury.

Chaos Space Marine units

The Aspiring Champion (if any) gains the Sorcerer ability and will automatically pass any Psychic tests taken; the rest of the unit receives the Rubric Sign identifying them as members of the Thousand Sons Legion. Models with the Rubric Sign are gifted with the Daemonic Essence ability. In addition they follow the Slow and Purposeful special rule. They are not affected by the 'Gift of Chaos' and 'Mass Mutation' psychic powers as they have no true bodies to reshape.

Units with the Mark of Tzeentch may not take any Veteran skills; in the case of the characters, Sorcery demands their full attention, whereas models with the Rubric Sign are mindless automatons unable to learn.

Slow and Purposeful

Models with the Rubric Sign advance in a methodical manner laying down a constant hail of fire. To represent this they may always count as stationary when firing, even if they moved in the same turn.

They are slow however and move as if they were in difficult terrain when they are in open terrain, they never receive +1 Attack for charging, strike at Initiative 1 in close combat and may never choose to perform a Sweeping Advance.

Weaponry of the followers of Tzeentch

The following weapon upgrades are available to units with the Mark of Tzeentch.

Chosen.
No special restrictions.

Chaos Marines.
Apart from Aspiring Champions all models must use Bolters as their standard weaponry and cannot upgrade any weaponry unless they are upgraded to Terminators.

Any units may all be upgraded to Terminators at +18 points per model. They will replace their normal weaponry with power weapons and combi-bolters. Only the Aspiring Champion of the unit (if there is one) may further upgrade his weaponry. Any units upgraded in this way will count as Elite selections on the force organisation chart.

Vehicles of Tzeentch

A vehicle dedicated to Tzeentch has the Coruscating Flame ability. This costs +15 pts.

Coruscating Flame

The vehicle is covered in weird gargoyles that constantly chatter incantations, pausing only to exhale great clouds of warp fire. The vehicle is covered in a sheet of warp flame that consumes enemy troops.

Any model attacking the vehicle takes a Str D6, AP4 hit before resolving its attacks.

Armoury of Tzeentch

The following items are added to the main armoury but can only be selected by models with the Mark of Tzeentch. The normal restrictions by category of item stated in the main armoury section apply. Items marked with a * can be used by models in Terminator armour.

Bedlam Staff* (Daemon Weapon)	25 pts
Blasted Standard*	50 pts
Bolt of Change*	30 pts
Disc of Tzeentch	30 pts
Eye of Tzeentch*	20 pts
Inferno bolts*	10 pts
Minor Psychic Power*	10 pts
Talisman of Tzeentch*	5 pts
Thrall Wizard*	5 pts each
Twisting Path*	15 pts
Warp Blade* (Daemon Weapon)	25 pts

Bedlam Staff

The Thousand Sons Legion of Chaos Space Marines were powerful adepts before the Horus Heresy compelled them to serve Tzeentch. Their Sorcerers always used their staves as foci for their powers and the few staves that remain are steeped in ten millennia of wild psychic power. Enemy struck by it are temporarily dazed as its power drives conscious thought from their minds.

The Bedlam Staff is a Daemon Weapon that clouds the minds of those struck by it. A Bedlam Staff counts as a power weapon but any model wounded by it and not killed may not attack until the end of the next Assault phase. Vehicles hit by it are 'crew shaken' in addition to any other results they suffer.

Blasted Standard

Riddled with the power of change, the standard's design shifts constantly through the battle. Energy and power growl through it and when an enemy approaches it the energy is released in a blinding roar. In addition to acting as an icon for summoning Daemons, the standard contains a powerful spell that may be used once per battle in the Chaos player's Shooting phase instead of its bearer firing a weapon. It may be aimed at any enemy unit with a model within 6" of the Icon Bearer and may even target a unit in close combat. The spell inflicts 2D6 S6 AP4 hits.

Bolt of Change

The Bolt of Change is a psychic power that may be used in the model's Shooting phase instead of firing a weapon. When used, the Bolt of Change counts as a weapon with the following profile. Roll to hit, etc, as normal.

Range 24"   Str 8   AP 2   Assault 1

Eye of Tzeentch

The Champion bears a third eye either on his body or his wargear. The eye sees what will come to pass allowing the Champion to adjust his actions in time. The Eye allows the Champion to re-roll either a single armour save, a single to hit roll or a single to wound roll in each of their own turns.

Inferno bolts

Inferno bolts are sorcerous bolter, combi-bolter or bolt pistol shells that have been inscribed with arcane runes that writhe with blue-white fire. These bolts can be used instead of normal ammunition and confer the Blast ability to each shot, roll to hit as normal but place the small Blast marker to determine how many models are hit.

Tzeentch Minor Psychic Power

The model may make a single roll on the Tzeentch Minor Psychic Power table. Duplicate powers are re-rolled.

Disc of Tzeentch

Discs of Tzeentch are daemonic warp entities that soar on the etheric winds in the Eye of Terror. They are sometimes gifted to Tzeentch's faithful as Steeds. A Disc of Tzeentch confers the Daemonic Flight and Daemonic Mutation gifts upon its rider. Models with followers may not ride a Disc.

Talisman of Tzeentch

If an army includes a model with this talisman, opposing psykers suffer a -1 modifier to their Leadership for psychic tests. Multiple Talismans have no cumulative effect. If both sides have this gift they cancel each other out and the normal rules apply

Thrall Wizard

Follower. Thrall Wizards are normal human sorcerers that serve Chaos Sorcerers as apprentices. Only models with psychic abilities may have Thrall Wizards and each sorcerer can command up to 4 of them. Thrall Sorcerers may be sacrificed to allow their master to use more than one psychic power in a turn.

	WS	BS	S	T	W	I	A	Ld	Sv
Thrall Wizard	3	3	3	3	1	3	1	7	-

A Thrall Sorcerer may not be given weapons or Wargear.

When the Sorcerer wishes to use a further power a Thrall is sacrificed and the psychic power is cast automatically. No more than one Thrall Wizard can be sacrificed by the same Sorcerer in a turn. A Thrall Wizard may be sacrificed to use the same power a second time in the same turn.

Twisting Path

The Sorcerer is preparing the way for Tzeentch's Grand Design. The power is used in the Shooting phase instead of firing a weapon, has a range of 12" and requires line of sight. The target unit suffers an unsettling waking dream in which they betray their friends and ally themselves with the Dark Powers. Make a Leadership test for the unit; if they fail they are pinned until the start of the next Chaos turn. The power has no effect on models with no Leadership rating or which are immune to pinning.

The main effect of this spell is far greater though. While they are ensorcelled the Sorcerer pulls information from the targets' minds, establishes post-hypnotic suggestions to use later and alters their memories or perceptions to achieve some ineffable goal. Each time the Sorcerer successfully pins a unit with the Twisting Path he will earn 50 Victory Points for his side in missions using the Victory Points special rule. This Victory Point bonus can only be earned once per enemy unit per game.

Warp Blade

Gifted to the mightiest of sorcerers and most devious of plotters, the Warp Blade has the power to dissipate and scatter psychic energy aimed at its bearer. This tends to attract the denizens of the Warp who hungrily sniff out the source of the power.

Any enemy psyker using a psychic power when within 12" of the Warp Blade must roll a D6. On a 4+ the power works normally, otherwise they will suffer an immediate Perils of the Warp attack and the power will fail to function. If an enemy is killed in this way, it does not count as being killed by the daemon weapon for mastery purposes. The Warp Blade is a power weapon.

Tzeentch Minor Psyker Powers

1. No Usable Power
Effect: The psyker's patron pays no heed to his prayers. The roll is wasted.

2. Pink Fire Of Tzeentch
Phase: Own Shooting **Psychic Test?** No **Range:** 12"
Effect: Calling on his patron god, the psyker unleashes a torrent of Warp fire upon his foes. The psyker may make an attack as if they had the Daemonic Fire gift.

3. Psychic Duel
Phase: Own Shooting **Psychic Test?** No **Range:** Battlefield
Effect: Reaching with his mind across the battlefield, the psyker seeks to undermine the concentration of enemy psykers. Any power used by a specified enemy psyker in the next player turn that requires a psychic test will be at -1 Leadership. This modifier is cumulative with the effect of the Talisman of Tzeentch.

4. Reckoning Of Tzeentch
Phase: Own Shooting **Psychic Test?** No **Range:** Self
Effect: The psyker has received Tzeentch's blessings, reading the strands of fate as they unravel before him. The psyker and any squad he accompanies may re-roll missed to hit rolls this Shooting phase. As ever, a shot may only ever be re-rolled once, even if the weapon is master-crafted.

5. Weaver Of Fates
Phase: Not applicable **Psychic Test?** No **Range:** Battlefield
Effect: Tzeentch is often called the master of deceit, and his followers will try to gain his blessings when planning an attack. The Tzeentch player's strategy rating is 3; this may affect the choice of mission.

6. Withering Gaze
Phase: Enemy Assault **Psychic Test?** No **Range:** 6"
Effect: The psyker's eyes burn with a small portion of Tzeentch's own baleful gaze, causing his enemies to avert their own eyes as they attempt to engage him. This power forces the enemy to make a Leadership test if they wish to assault the psyker or any squad he has joined. If the enemy's test is failed, they may assault an alternative target if one is within range. Units which ignore or automatically pass Morale checks are unaffected by this power. This power may only be used if the psyker is not already fighting in an assault.

The Thousand Sons

An age ago, the Thousand Sons were counted amongst the most loyal of the Emperor's Legions, but that all ended when their sorcerous Primarch Magnus the Red attempted to utilise forbidden magics in order to warn the Emperor of Horus's treachery.

Cast out by the Imperium, the Thousand Sons now reside in a place of twisted sorcery from where they travel out into the galaxy to gather slaves for their magical experiments.

The majority of the Legion are mindless automatons, made soulless by their Chief Librarian's spell to rid them of the mutations caused by their exposure to the raw stuff of Chaos. Now these silent, relentless enemies of the Imperium are led into battle by the mightiest of sorcerers; individuals wholly dedicated to Tzeentch, the Lord of Sorcery.

Playing a Thousand Sons army

If you want to use a pure Thousand Sons army you must adhere to the following limitations:

- All characters and units must have the Mark of Tzeentch. Characters or units that cannot have the Mark of Tzeentch cannot be used.
- The only Daemons that can be used are those belonging to Tzeentch.
- Vehicles may only be dedicated to Tzeentch although they may be undedicated.
- Any Favoured unit allowed Aspiring Champions may upgrade one model to an Aspiring Champion for free.
- Favoured Daemon Packs or Daemonic Beasts units may add +1 to their summoning roll.

Ahriman of the Thousand Sons

It was inevitable that Ahriman, the Chief Librarian of the Thousand sons would be drawn to the mystic lore gathered at their Primarch, Magnus the Red's, command during the great crusade. Magnus's obsessions were his and like Magnus, Ahriman studied every piece of knowledge so that the Thousand Sons would be able to harness the power of the warp for their own purposes. Their fascination with mysticism gradually turned the Thousand Sons from being the Emperors warriors to self-obsessed Sorcerers. Ultimately the Emperor had to act and unleashed the Space Wolves against them.

Broken by the savagery of the Space Wolves the remaining Thousand Sons had little option to take refuge with Horus and further dedicate themselves to Tzeentch. Soon though, the Thousand Sons began to suffer the effects of debilitating mutation. Ahriman stepped to the fore to convene a conclave of the mightiest sorcerers. He secured their aid in performing a spell he called the Rubric of Ahriman that would halt the mutating effect of Chaos. The spell was cast, those Thousand Sons with sorcerous powers survived it with their powers augmented, those without sorcerous powers were reduced to dust, their spirits trapped inside their armour for all eternity. Ahriman held the Rubric to be a success as the physical corruption had been halted even at a cost of changing most of the Legion to automata.

Ahriman and his cabal were exiled from the Planet of the Sorcerers for their actions, condemned to wander the cosmos in a search for perfect understanding. Since then they have sought out magical artefacts, ancient tomes and talented psykers across the galaxy. Their threat is such that many members of the Inquisition would rather destroy an artefact than risk it falling into the hands of Ahriman's Cabal.

	Points	WS	BS	S	T	W	I	A	Ld	Sv
Ahriman	215	5	5	4	4	3	5	3	10	3+

Any Thousand Sons army may be led by Ahriman. If you take him then he counts as the Chaos Lord choice for the army. He must be used exactly as described below and may not be given extra equipment from the Chaos Armoury although he may be accompanied by a retinue of Chosen selected in the normal way.

Wargear and Gifts: Bolt pistol with Inferno bolts, frag & krak grenades, Black Staff of Ahriman, Mark of Tzeentch & Talisman of Tzeentch.

Psychic Powers: Bolt of Change, The Twisting Path, Doom Bolt, Gift of Chaos, Wind of Chaos, Mass mutation.

SPECIAL RULES

Master of Sorcery: Over the centuries Ahriman has stolen the secrets of his sorcerous opponents. He is therefore able to make a single roll on any one of the Minor Psychic Powers and Chaos Minor Psychic Powers tables of your choice, before the game begins.

The Black Staff of Ahriman: The Black Staff is a potent focus of psychic energy. Whenever Ahriman uses a psychic power roll a D6. On a roll of 4+ he may use a psychic power again in the same turn and may re-use the same power if he desires. If Ahriman succeeds in using a psychic power for a second time (ie, he rolls a 4+), then he may go for further attempts, but these subsequent attempts will only work on a D6 roll of 6. As soon as Ahriman fails a dice roll he may no longer use any psychic powers that turn, but may use them again normally in his next turn. Because of the power of the staff Ahriman disdains the use of Thrall Wizards and Familiars.

Independent Character: Ahriman is an independent character and follows all the independent character special rules as given in the Warhammer 40,000 rulebook.

THE RISE TO DAEMONHOOD OF THE DAEMON PRINCE PERICLITOR,
IN THE WORDS OF ONE WHO WALKED IN HIS SHADOW

THE CASTILE V MASSACRE - 832.M33
Upon the slaughter fields of fair Castile did our lord Periclitor first seal his pact with the powers of the Warp. A thousand souls were tossed to the Empyrean that day. Most savoured of all were the Missionarius and the Sororitas, whose soul-screams still ease our sleep each night.

THE MARTYRDOM OF SAINT JEROME - 888.M33
Known to the servants of the False Emperor as Jerome the Pure, known to us as Jerome the Fool, Jerome the Blind. At Tosak, he sought to challenge Periclitor, and there along with his host we ran him to ground. We put Jerome to death, but only after each of his followers in turn had been eviscerated before his very eyes.

ALCMENA NEBULA WARS - 012.M34
A word in an ear, a coin in a palm and a hundred thousand throw themselves upon the crucible of war. By his own hand did man draw the blood sacrifice, and Periclitor was holding the vessel that received it.

THE LAST STAND OF THE 5TH ARMOURED TERRAN PRAEFECTS - 739.M35
If the False Emperor will man tanks with scribes and clerks then we shall fill graves with fools and hypocrites.

THE SENTRY VAULT INCIDENT - 799.M36
Savants and scholars have for centuries ruminated upon the contents of the Sentry Vault. Now they shall never know, for Periclitor led an army of his favoured upon the sacred ground of Urus Prime. The Treacher Inquisition sent forth its finest, the grey clad hunters of our kin, but within the inner sanctum of the vault itself our lord bested them, earning the favour of our masters.

AMBUSH OF CHAPTER MASTER ORLANDO FURIOSO OF THE HOWLING GRIFFONS AT ARIOS POINT - 220.M38
Late in the year 220.M38, word reached Periclitor that the Howling Griffons Chapter were preparing to celebrate the 5000th anniversary of their Founding; it seemed only fitting he should mark the occasion with the reverence it deserved. As Furioso and the First Company made their way to the Chapter's homeworld, our lord and a substantial force of his Chosen fell upon the Howling Griffons' ship as it traversed the Arios Beacon. The battle was a furious one, culminating with Periclitor and his elite boarding Furioso's battle barge aboard their Dreadclaws. The attack crippled the ship, and the defenders were forced to evacuate aboard their Thunderhawks and escape pods. The battle was continued upon the surface of Arios Quintus, where the survivors were surrounded and butchered in short order. The body of Furioso was mounted upon the fore of his Thunderhawk and its transponders set to transmit its location to any who entered the system. The remainder of the Chapter found it a month later, and now have another date to mark in their calendar each year.

THE CORRUPTION OF THE SANCTITY IX PEDAGOGUE - 273.M38
How the dark powers mocked the night the Pedagogue fell! That one so certain in their faith and teachings may be turned gives hope to us all that the servants of the False Emperor may not be so deaf to our preachings.

THE MURDER OF THE CARDINAL OF BRAY - 789.M38
Upon the eve of Candlemass, 789.M38, Periclitor was gifted with a great vision of things to come. Chaos in all its undiluted glory spoke directly to him, promising the gift of Daemonhood should he continue to serve. Seeking the blessings of our patrons, he acted immediately, launching a surprise assault upon the nearby world of Bray. We teleported directly to the Cathedral itself. The Cardinal was giving his Candlemass Day sermon to the massed subjects of his false doctrine. Our lord materialised directly behind the Cardinal as he reached the end of his address, and plunged his blade through his heart. As the congregation erupted in panic we departed, leaving none upon Bray in any doubt as to our ability to strike whenever, and wherever we pleased.

INCITEMENT OF THE BRAUN IV TITHE WARS - 187.M39
The Tithe Wars saw Periclitor elevated to the rank of Daemonhood, for which we all give praise to our masters. The murder of the Cardinal of Bray had set about a chain of events that, three centuries later culminated in the entire sector rebelling against the weakling rule of Terra. When we attacked Bray, we had demonstrated that the planet's defences were completely inadequate, a situation that its self-righteous leaders sought to remedy immediately through the imposition of a tax that would raise the funds to build an extensive orbital defence. Each time a new tithe was presented before the world's ruling committee, it was rejected; and so we would attack once more, forcing the committee to accept the higher expenditure necessary to halt our predations. In time the populace could pay no more, and first Bray, and then the entire Trans-Kurani sub-sector erupted in civil war. Soon the entire sector was embroiled in the war, with Imperial Guard regiments, Space Marine companies and Imperial Navy fleets brought in to quell the rebellion.

At the height of the blessed conflict, which rages to this day in some areas, Periclitor received his promised reward. Standing in triumph atop the ruins of the Cathedral of Bray, he was lifted to the sky within a nimbus of black light. Minutes later he was returned to us transformed and bearing the full gifts of his apotheosis. His face was a bestial mask, his arms were enlarged to the size of cannon barrels, and upon his back were two black wings, fully five metres across when spread.

Under such a being, how could we fail in our service to the dark powers of Chaos?

CHAOS SPACE MARINES SUMMARY

	WS	BS	S	T	W	I	A	Ld	Sv
Chaos Lord	5	5	4	4	3	5	3	10	3+
Chaos Champion	5	5	4	4	2	5	3	10	3+
Chosen	4	4	4	4	1	4	1	10	3+
Chosen Terminator	4	4	4	4	1	4	2	10	2+/5+*
Chosen Aspiring Champion	4	4	4	4	1	4	2	10	3+
Chosen Terminator Champion	4	4	4	4	1	4	3	10	2+/5+*
Possessed	4	4	5	4	1	4	1	10	3+/5+*
Possessed Aspiring Champion	4	4	5	4	1	4	2	10	3+/5+*
Obliterator	4	4	5	5	2	4	2	9	2+/5+*
Chaos Space Marine	4	4	4	4	1	4	1	9	3+
Aspiring Champion	4	4	4	4	1	4	2	10	3+
Chaos Biker	4	4	4(5)	1	4	2	9	3+
Chaos Biker Aspiring Champion	4	4	4(5)	1	4	3	10	3+
Raptor	4	4	4	4	1	4	1	9	3+
Raptor Aspiring Champion	4	4	4	4	1	4	2	10	3+
Bloodthirster	9	0	8	6	4	4	5	10	3+/4+*
Great Unclean One	5	3	7	6	6	2	3	10	-/4+*
Lord of Change	8	4	6	6	4	6	3	10	-/4+*
Keeper of Secrets	7	3	7	6	4	4	5	10	-/4+*
Bloodletter	4	0	5	4	1	4	2	10	3/5+*
Plaguebearer	4	0	4	4(5)	1	4	2	8	-/5+*
Horror	2	3	4	3	2	2	1	8	-/5+*
Daemonette	4	0	4	3	1	4	2	8	-/5+*
Nurglings	3	0	3	3	3	3	3	7	5+
Flesh Hound	4	0	5	4	1	5	2	8	-/5+*
Screamer	4	0	4	4	1	5	1	8	-/5+*
Furies	4	0	5	4	1	5	2	7	-/5+*

Indicates an Invulnerable save.

	WS	BS	S	Front	Side	Rear	I	A
				Armour				
Dreadnought	4	4	6(10)	12	12	10	4	3
Defiler	2	4	8	12	12	10	4	2
Chaos Rhino	–	4	–	11	11	10	–	–
Chaos Predator	–	4	–	13	11	10	–	–
Chaos Land Raider	–	4	–	14	14	14	–	–

Weapon	Range	Str	AP	Type
Bolt Pistol	12"	4	5	Pistol
Plasma Pistol	12"	7	2	Pistol, Gets hot
Bolter	24"	4	5	Rapid Fire
Combi-Bolter	24"	4	5	Rapid Fire, twin-linked
Heavy Bolter	36"	5	4	Heavy 3
Flamer	Template	4	5	Assault 1, No cover save
Plasma Gun	24"	7	2	Rapid Fire; Gets hot
Melta Gun	12"	8	1	Assault 1, +D6 armour pen. within 6"
Autocannon	48"	7	4	Heavy 2
Lascannon	48"	9	2	Heavy 1
Heavy Flamer	Template	5	4	Assault 1, No Cover Save
Missile Launcher (Frag)	48"	4	6	Heavy 1, Blast
Missile Launcher (Krak)	48"	8	3	Heavy 1
Reaper Autocannon	36"	7	4	Heavy 2, Twin-linked
Doom Siren	Template	4	5	Assault 1, No Cover Save
Sonic Blaster	24"	4	5	Assault 2 or Heavy 3
Blastmaster (varied frequency)	36"	5	5	Assault 2, Causes Pinning
Blastmaster (single frequency)	36"	8	4	Heavy 1, Blast
Battle cannon	72" or	8	3	Ordnance1/Blast
	G36"-72"	8	3	Barrage, Causes Pinning

Chainfist: Strikes last; doubles strength; 2D6 + Strength for Armour Penetration
Combi-bolter: Twin-linked bolter
Combi-flamer: Fire as flamer once per battle; bolter at all other times
Combi-melta: Fire as meltagun once per battle; bolter at all other times
Great weapon: +1 Strength; requires two hands.
Lightning Claws: Power weapon; re-roll failed to wound rolls; bonus attack only when using as a pair.
Bionics: Ignore final wound on a roll of 6
Chaos Hound: Follower. See rules.
Chaos Space Marine Bike: Steed. Moves as Bike; +1 Toughness; +1 Attack.
Master crafted weapon: Re-roll one miss with that weapon per turn.
Personal Icon: Personal Icon can be used as a focus for Daemon Summoning.
Spiky Bits: Re-roll one miss in each round of close combat.
Teleport homer: Teleporting troops centred on bearer will not scatter.
Terminator Armour: 2+ armour save; 5+ invulnerable save; +1 Attack; move and fire with heavy weapons.

SPECIAL ICONS
Daemon Icon: One unit of Daemons summoned automatically.
Icon of Chaos Undivided: Summon Daemons; models with Mark of Chaos Undivided within 6" are Fearless

PSYCHIC ABILITIES AND EQUIPMENT
Doombolt: Psychic power; Range 18" Strength 5 AP 4 Assault 3
Familiar: Owner may have two major psychic powers
Gift of Chaos: Target model in 2"; roll D6; if greater than target's Toughness (or 6) target becomes Chaos Spawn.
Mass Mutation: Target friendly unit joined by sorceror; gain random ability (see p.18)
Sorcerer: Character is allowed to cast spells and buy psychic gifts.
Warp Focus: Adds D6" to the range of psychic power projected through it except Wind of Chaos. Roll for additional range each time a power is used.
Warp Talisman: Sorcerer can re-roll a Psychic Power Test once per battle.
Wind of Chaos: Psychic test; place flamer; affected models wounded on 4+; invulnerable saves only.

DAEMONIC GIFTS
Daemon Armour: 2+ armour save
Daemonic Aura: 5+ Invulnerable save
Daemonic Chains: Re-roll dice for Daemon Possession
Daemonic Essence: +1 Wound
Daemonic Fire: Shooting attack: Range 12" Str 4 AP6 Assault 2
Daemon Flight: Move as if equipped with Jump Pack
Daemonic Mutation: +1 Attack
Daemonic Resilience: +1 Toughness
Daemonic Rune: No instant death
Daemonic Stature: +1 Strength; +1 Toughness; Monstrous Creature
Daemon Steed: Move as cavalry; Daemonic resilience
Daemon Spawn: Follower; See rules for profile
Daemonic Speed: Move as Cavalry
Daemonic Strength: +1 Strength
Daemonic Talons: Gives additional close combat weapon bonus; roll of 6 to hit auto wound, no armour save; roll bonus dice on Armour Penetration roll of 6
Daemon Venom: Wounds on 4+, unless roll would be less normally
Daemonic Visage: Defeated enemy in close combat at -1 Ld (-2 if Greater Daemon or all have Daemonic Visage) for Morale checks

VETERAN ABILITIES
Counter-Attack: Unengaged models may move up to 6" to contact enemy
Furious Charge: Models gain +1 Initiative and +1 Strength when charging
Infiltrate: Squad may use Infiltrators scenario special rule if allowed by scenario
Move Through Cover: Roll extra D6 when rolling for difficult terrain
Night Vision: May re-roll dice when checking vision under Night Fighing rules
Siege Specialists: +1 on any penetration rolls against bunkers and tank traps; only trigger minefields on a roll of 6; Fearless when defending fortifications
Skilled Riders: Re-roll any 1's rolled for dangerous terrain tests
Tank Hunters: Always pass Morale checks due to tank shock; +1 to all armour penetration rolls with heavy or special weapons, melta-bombs and krak grenades

DAEMON WEAPONS
Dark Blade: +2 Strength for to wound rolls or armour penetration rolls.
Dreadaxe: Wounds on 4+, unless roll would be less normally; no invulnerable saves.
Ether Lance: Power weapon; shoots with the following profile.

Range:Template	Str 4	AP3	Assault 1

Kai Gun: One-handed if bearer has Daemonic Stature, otherwise two-handed

Range: 24"	Str 6	AP3	Assault 2

Mark of Nurgle: Fearless; Daemonic Resilience (+1 Toughness); True Grit

Mark of Khorne: Fearless; +1 Attack; must charge enemy in range; roll D6 at start of Movement phase - move towards enemy extra D6" and may not shoot on a 1 or 2; always sweeping advance

Mark of Slaanesh: Warp Scream (enemy in close combat at -1 Initiative); Fearless

Mark of Tzeentch (Characters and Aspiring Chmpions): Sorcerer; always pass Psychic tests.

Mark of Tzeentch (Chaos Space Marine units): Fearless; Daemonic Essence; Slow and Purposeful; no Veteran abilities

The Daemon Prince Dhar'leth leads his Black Legion army across the blasted surface of Antecanis IV

One of the attractions of collecting a Chaos Space Marine army is watching it grow from a small warband to a much larger force. Under the command of an Aspiring Champion of the Chaos powers, the warband will expand to become an all-conquering horde capable of challenging both the lackeys of the False Emperor and any warlord standing in your way.

WHERE TO BEGIN

The Chaos Space Marine army has a lot to offer when it comes to selecting your force. From the heavy weaponry of the Havocs to the monstrously powerful Greater Daemons, the Chaos Space Marines are able to field an enormous range of troop types, characters and war machines. Each has its own strengths and weaknesses, abilities and specialisations on the battlefield, and choosing which to take can be tough. The best thing to do first is pick a 'core' force and build your army from there. This means you'll quickly be able to get your models on the table, ready to play some games.

When choosing which units to pick, you should bear in mind the force organisation charts as these dictate which type of units and how many of each you'll be able to field. The best one to start with is the chart for Standard Missions, which allows you to pick a tactically flexible force that can be easily expanded into a larger army.

As you can see from the chart, a force chosen from the Standard Missions force organisation chart must have at least one HQ and two Troops units, so it's a good idea to start collecting these first. Once you have this core force painted, you'll be ready to play some games. From here you can expand your army to play more varied scenarios and include some specialised units.

The different elements of a Chaos Space Marine army need to work together to be successful and, as your army expands, you'll learn what works best for your style of play. Soon you'll be leading your ruthless warband to victory after victory in the eternal war.

STANDARD MISSIONS

COMPULSORY	OPTIONAL
1 HQ	1 HQ
2 Troops	4 Troops
	3 Elites
	3 Fast Attack
	3 Heavy Support

HQ · ELITES

TROOPS · TROOPS · FAST ATTACK · HEAVY SUPPORT

A core Chaos force made up of two squads of Chaos Space Marines (Troops) and a Chaos Lord (HQ).

A large number of the models in your army will be made up from the Chaos Space Marines plastic boxed set, which allows for an enormous amount of variety. On this page we'll give you some tips on assembling your Chaos Space Marines, and show you how we painted our Black Legion models.

We've found that before gluing the model, it's a good idea to try out the pose first, sticking the pieces together using Blu-Tac. The Chaos Space Marines set comes with a lot of extra details and we glued these on last to ensure the main components fitted together.

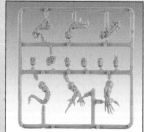

The plastic Chaos Space Marines boxed set comes complete with a set of Chaos Mutations, which you can use to make complete squads of Possessed, or just to add variety to your Chaos Space Marine squads.

The parts on the Chaos Mutations sprue replace parts of the Chaos Space Marines; simply use a mutated head in place of a helmet, or a tentacle instead of an arm and your squads will appear especially gifted by their Chaos patrons.

We undercoated our assembled Black Legionnaire using Chaos Black spray paint. We then applied Chainmail to the boltgun and banding on the model's arms, legs and helmet. To give the Black Legionnaire an ornate yet simple look, we applied Shining Gold to the banding on the shoulder pads, the arrow on the helmet and also the boltgun. All that was left to paint on our model then was the topknot, which we painted with Red Gore. After basing the Black Legionnaire he was ready for gaming.

Drybrushing is a quick method for highlighting your models, particularly ones with lots of textured or metal parts such as this Iron Warrior. For the main colour, we dipped the end of the brush in Boltgun Metal and then wiped away most of the paint onto a tissue. We then lightly brushed across the model, catching any raised areas.

Ink washes are used to quickly shade your models. For this World Eater, we used Red Ink, slightly darker than the model's Blood Red base coat. After applying a light wash over the model, we allowed it to seep into the recesses. Be careful not to use too much, as inks can take quite a while to dry.

TRANSFERS AND MARKINGS

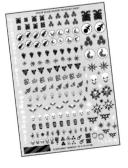

Transfers provide a quick and easy way of applying Legion iconography to the models of your army, without having to paint numerous individual markings. They also provide a way of identifying separate squads within your army and individuals within a squad.

BLACK LEGION   KHORNE   NURGLE   SLAANESH   TZEENTCH

Once you have your two Troops and one HQ choice, you're ready to begin expanding your army. Many players like to do this by collecting at least one new unit of each in the other categories in the force organisation chart.

THE ARMY GROWS

Once you've painted your core force and played a few games with it, you'll probably want to add more models and fight larger battles. There are a lot of different and varied units to choose from in the Chaos Space Marines list, and they all have their own strengths. In this section, we'll give you some guidance about the best way to expand your Chaos Space Marine army.

We've found that a good way of expanding a new army is to pick a selection from each of the other categories in the force organisation chart – Elites, Fast Attack and Heavy Support. This way your army can grow quickly whilst remaining flexible enough to handle itself in any mission or against any army.

The Chaos Space Marines army list is very flexible, allowing you to tailor your force to your own style of play. You could theme your army towards a rapid assault, mounting one or more squads in a Rhino, and adding a squad of Chaos Terminators, a Land Raider and a pack of Furies, as in the photo below. Alternatively, you might prefer a force with a lot of mobile, heavy firepower, by choosing a Chaos Predator, a Chaos Space Marine Bike squadron and an Obliterator Cult instead.

As the lord of a Chaos Space Marine army, you have at your disposal a fearsome array of wargear, troops and abilities. If your preferred method of winning is to tear your enemy apart in a brutal and decisive assault, then Possessed Chaos Space Marines or Khorne Berzerkers are a good way of expanding your army. If you prefer to engage your opponent from a distance, only moving in for the kill when the moment is ideal, then perhaps Noise Marines are for you. The Chaos Space Marines army list caters for an enormous range of playing styles, with the various Legion-specific rules allowing further specialisation. Of course the main list, which represents the tactically flexible force of the Black Legion, is the most open and a good basis for those just setting out on the path to Chaos.

How you prefer to fight your battles will play a large part in your selections, and after a few games you'll soon discover what suits you best. Whatever style of play you favour, the Chaos Space Marine army can be tailored to fight in that manner so it's completely up to you how you use it.

HEAVY SUPPORT

FAST ATTACK

TROOPS

HQ

ELITES

TROOPS

The original core force has been expanded to include a Rhino transport for one squad, a Chaos Terminator squad (Elites), a Land Raider (Heavy Support) and a pack of Furies (Fast Attack).

CHAOS SPACE MARINE TACTICS

Once you have your army ready for battle, you'll want to fight and win with it. Learning how to use your army is part of the pleasure of playing Warhammer 40,000, and to help you wreak vengeance upon the Imperium, we'll illustrate some effective tactics for using your Chaos Space Marine army.

CHAOS DREADNOUGHT

Well-armed for shooting or fighting, the Dreadnought should attempt to use whichever method suits the enemy least. When defending, it is strong enough to deter enemy assaults against nearby friends and on the offensive it can fire as it advances. As a Walker it has the advantage over other vehicles in that it can advance safely through difficult terrain. It is the ideal weapon to provide close support for your infantry.

CHAOS SPACE MARINES

This squad is fighting on foot. Chaos Space Marines are excellent all-round troops so the unit can be used either to attack or defend. On the attack, it is best used to support the charge of a more powerful unit such as the Khorne Berzerkers or the Dreadnought; on the defence, use it to prevent the enemy getting at your own specialist shooting units such as the Havocs or Predator.

CHAOS HAVOCS

Havocs have a wide choice of heavy weapons and can be armed in such a way that, whatever target presents itself, they have a good weapon for dealing with it. They cannot move and fire though, so it is important to get them into a good position to shoot from as quickly as possible and to keep them behind the rest of the army so that they cannot easily be charged.

CHAOS PREDATOR

The Predator can move 6" and fire its twin-linked lascannon or remain static and fire all its weaponry. Lascannons are very powerful weapons and should, as a preference, be used to deal with the enemy's heavy tanks.

CHAOS BIKERS

Bikes are fast and, in addition, their riders get an extra attack. Their combi-bolters can target an enemy at long range even while moving and they can be upgraded to flamers, meltaguns or plasma guns. This makes Chaos Bikes a very flexible troop type that will have some way of damaging virtually anything. They should use cover as they advance, as they are too expensive in points to expose to the enemy's guns unnecessarily.

DAEMONS

Unknown to the enemy there are Daemons in reserve waiting to be summoned during the game!

FURIES

Furies are winged Daemons of Chaos Undivided. Their additional mobility makes them a potent threat, able to attack the enemy directly or act in support of the army's more mobile units.

BLOODLETTERS

Bloodletters are the footsoldiers of Khorne. Their unexpected arrival can easily turn the tide of battle, especially if summoned close to the enemy where they can put their deadly Hellblades to best effect.

CHAOS LORD

This squad is mounted in a Rhino and accompanied by the Chaos Lord. The Rhino doubles the unit's speed and provides protection when crossing open ground. The Chaos Lord and unit Aspiring Champion are very powerful in close assault so this unit can either lead the attack, or be used to counter-attack enemies assaulting the Chaos lines.

KHORNE BERZERKERS

Although they are fighting on foot, the Berzerkers' Blood Rage ability makes them capable of a very fast charge. As they fight in a frenzy with massive chainaxes, they not only get more attacks than other troops but reduce the effectiveness of the best enemy armour. Berzerkers should attack immediately, using cover to reduce losses as they close in but without slowing them down too much.

Daemons of all varieties provide a particularly Chaotic focus for your army. The Bloodthirster, Great Unclean One, Lord of Change and Keeper of Secrets are all highly characterful models, and hopefully these pages will provide some ideas to get you started painting them and their Lesser Daemon minions.

The colours of Khorne are red and black, and these Daemons have been painted Blood Red and Chaos Black, complemented with Brazen Brass and Bleached Bone.

Suggested colours:

■	Blood Red	■	Brazen Brass
■	Chaos Black	□	Bleached Bone

The use of gloss varnish is the perfect way to give your Daemons of Nurgle a really disgusting, slime-covered finish.

Suggested colours:

■	Camo Green	■	Bronzed Flesh
■	Snakebite Leather	■	Boltgun Metal

These servants of Slaanesh are painted in pale colours that provide a contrast to the Chaos Black of their garments.

Suggested colours:

⬜ Skull White	⬛ Red Gore
⬛ Chaos Black	⬜ Chainmail

Colours such as Liche Purple and Regal Blue are ideal for the Daemons of Tzeentch, with details picked out in Skull White and Fiery Orange.

Suggested colours:

⬜ Skull White	⬛ Regal Blue
⬛ Liche Purple	⬛ Fiery Orange

WORLD EATERS

The World Eaters are a legion of deadly warriors who live for only one purpose: to slay in the name of the Blood God. If you choose an army of these insane psychopaths you will be rewarded with a force that is straightforward to play with and offers you a wealth of conversion opportunities.

The colours of the World Eaters are those of Khorne, and these warriors are painted Blood Red, with details picked out in Shining Gold.

Suggested colours:

- Blood Red
- Chaos Black
- Shining Gold
- Boltgun Metal

DEATH GUARD

The Plague Marines of the Death Guard are the favoured of Nurgle, bearing the dubious gifts of their repulsive patron. On the tabletop, you can rely on your Plague Marines to receive a charge from the most hard-hitting of foes without falling, and few opponents will be able to resist the inevitable counter-attack that follows.

These Plague Marines have been painted with mixes of colours such as Snakebite Leather, Camo Green and Bronzed Flesh.

Suggested colours:

- Bestial Brown
- Bleached Bone
- Chaos Black
- Chaos Black
- Snot Green
- Snakebite Leather
- Bronzed Flesh
- Camo Green

EMPEROR'S CHILDREN

An Emperor's Children warband is a riot of garish colours. If your ideal army is a combination of graceful yet deadly close combat specialists and devastating medium range armaments, then these servants of Slaanesh are the force for you.

These Emperor's Children were painted with Tentacle Pink and Chaos Black, providing a strong contrast between the colours.

Suggested colours:

Tentacle Pink	Chaos Black
Chainmail	Rotting Flesh

THOUSAND SONS

The Thousand Sons are the progeny of Magnus the Red, the mystic Primarch who led his Legion of sorcerers against the Emperor during the Horus Heresy. To lead an army of them on the tabletop is to field an implacable force able to soak up an enormous amount of enemy firepower, whilst dealing out vast torrents of their own.

These models were painted Regal Blue, with Shining Gold and Golden Yellow detailing.

Suggested colours:

Regal Blue	Shining Gold
Golden Yellow	Bleached Bone

WORD BEARERS

The Word Bearers worship Chaos as a pantheon of the Dark Gods, making a cruel mockery of the Imperial Creed. The Legion can field more Daemons than any other Chaos Space Marine force and has access to unique blasphemous gifts and skills.

The crimson armour of these Word Bearers was achieved by applying a Magenta Ink wash to a Red Gore base coat.

Suggested colours:

- Red Gore
- Chainmail
- Magenta Ink
- Bleached Bone

IRON WARRIORS

The Iron Warriors excel at siege warfare. As an Iron Warriors player you get to field more Heavy Support choices than any other army, and even have access to two special vehicles: the Basilisk and the Vindicator.

These Iron Warriors' armour has been painted Boltgun Metal, with the banding picked out in Shining Gold.

Suggested colours:

- Boltgun Metal
- Shining Gold
- Chaos Black
- Sunburst Yellow

NIGHT LORDS

The Night Lords are consummate masters of the art of terror. On the tabletop they are a highly mobile army, able to make rapid strikes at isolated enemy units then redeploying before your opponent can react to the threat.

The Regal Blue of this Night Lord's armour is contrasted with Shining Gold on the banding and Blood Red on the top-knot.

Suggested colours:

■	Regal Blue	■	Shining Gold
■	Red Gore	■	Boltgun Metal

ALPHA LEGION

Operating far behind Imperial lines, the Alpha Legion sow discord and rebellion within the very borders of the Imperium. As an Alpha Legion player, you have access to the most stealthy of troops, able to infiltrate your opponent's army and wreak havoc amongst his units.

The colours of the Alpha Legion are blue and green. On this model, Regal Blue and Goblin Green have been blended together.

Suggested colours:

■	Storm Blue	■	Goblin Green
■	Blue Ink	■	Chainmail

SPACE MARINE RENEGADES

The Legions previously displayed are not the only Chaos Space Marines waging war against the Imperium. Inventing your own Legion, with its own colour scheme, history and identity can be a highly rewarding endeavour, and hopefully the ideas on this page will inspire you to do just that.

A Red Corsair formerly of the Dark Angels chapter.

A Red Corsair formerly of the Space Wolves chapter

Inventing your own renegade Chaos Space Marine Chapter provides an ideal opportunity to combine elements of the Space Marine and Chaos Space Marine plastic kits, along with other components from both ranges. The squad pictured here is formerly of the Crimson Fists Chapter but has joined the piratical Red Corsairs. It features defaced Chapter livery with a range of Chaotic conversions.

The Pyre
- Blazing Orange
- Chaos Black

Steel Cobras
- Brazen Brass
- Dark Angels Green

Children of Purgatos
- Snot Green
- Shining Gold

Warp Ghosts
- Rotting Flesh
- Chaos Black

Extinction Angels
- Liche Purple
- Bleached Bone

Violators
- Ultramarines Blue
- Chainmail

The Damned Company of Lord Caustos
- Fortress Grey
- Liche Purple

Sons of Malice
- Skull White
- Chaos Black

PAINTING CHAOS VEHICLES

A wide variety of vehicles are used by the Traitor Legions and, just like the Chaos Space Marines themselves, many share a common heritage with their loyalist counterparts. The Chaos hatch sprue and Chaos Spiky sprue both allow you to customise your armoured vehicles, giving them a uniquely Chaotic character and enhancing the overall personality of your army.

This vehicle has been adorned with a wide range of accessories from the Chaos hatch sprue.

These gun barrels are from the Chaos hatch sprue.

The trophy racks from the Chaos hatch sprue can be mounted on most areas of any Chaos vehicle.

The driver and pintle-mounted combi-bolter, or combi-flamer can be fitted into either of the top hatches of the Land Raider or Rhino.

Iron Warriors vehicles have a heavy, industrial appearance, which reflects the character of the Legion itself. Painting yellow and black stripes looks visually striking against the metallic hull.

To show that this is the transport vehicle for a squad of Khorne Berzerkers belonging to the Black Legion, details have been picked out in the characteristic red of the Blood God, as well as in the blood spattering its blades.

Details on Iron Warriors vehicles can be picked out in gold, contrasting with the silver.

The Destroyer vehicle gift on this Rhino was made using parts from the Ork Dreadnought – there are plenty of components from other models that can be used for conversions in this way.

CHAOS TERRAIN

Gaming with a well-painted army on a well-crafted battlefield is one of the most satisfying aspects of Warhammer 40,000. Themed terrain can serve as the backdrop for a single battle or an entire campaign, and can also provide inspiration for special scenarios of your own devising.

The Chaos Spiky sprue can be used to add the unmistakable taint of Chaos to your themed terrain.

You can make simple pieces of Chaos themed scenery out of items from your bits box as well as pieces you might find around the house. To make these trophy stakes, we collected a mass of spare plastic sprues and assorted leftover bits from other miniatures. These can be assembled in any way you see fit; here we used the plastic sprues to represent iron struts, and adorned these with heads and other parts of various models.

A Chaos army in all its glory, deployed on terrain especially designed and constructed to complement it, means your games and campaigns will be all the more engaging and memorable for your extra thought and effort.

CHAOS ARMY SHOWCASE

When you've assembled and painted your squads and vehicles, lavished extra attention on your characters and Daemons, and constructed a themed tabletop, you will appreciate just how worthwhile collecting a Chaos Space Marine army can be. This page features a massive force of Iron Warriors, comprising several members of the Studio staff's own armies.

A mighty Iron Warriors army besieges a doomed Imperial city.

SHOWCASE

These models are painted by the 'Eavy Metal team and by entrants to the illustrious Golden Demon contest. They illustrate just how worthwhile it is giving characters a really special treatment.

Chaos Lord,
painted by American Golden Demon 2000 award winner, Victor Hardy.

Chaos Dreadnought,
painted by Canadian Golden Demon 2001 award winner, Victor Hardy.

Ahriman, Chief Librarian of the Thousand Sons,
painted by Kirsten Mickelburgh.

Chaos Lord,
painted by French Golden Demon 2001 award winner, Jacques-Alexandre Gillois.

Abaddon the Despoiler,
painted by Spanish Golden Demon 2001 award winner, Jose Luis Roig Ayuso.

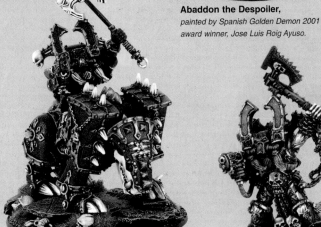

Daemon Prince destroying Dreadnought,
painted by French Golden Demon 2001 award winner, Jerôme Manouvrier.

An Aspiring Champion of Khorne mounted on a Juggernaut,
painted by Tammy Haye.

Kharn the Betrayer, Champion of Khorne.